JOCKS IN CHIEF

Forty-Four Essays Ranking the Most Athletic Presidents, from the Fight Crazy to the Spectacularly Lazy

JON FINKEL

Book Design by: Clark Kenyon
Cover Design by: Jeanine Henning
Editor: Jared Evans

"*Sports are good for the soul, good for life.*"
—George H. W. Bush

"*Move or die is the language of our Maker in the constitution of our bodies.*"
—John Adams

"*I was a fat band boy…*"
—Bill Clinton

TABLE OF CONTENTS

INTRODUCTION

Only 44 men in the history of the United States can relate to the pressure of a decision like sending in Seal Team Six to take out Osama bin Laden, whereas most of us everyday citizens relate to something more along the lines of saving two strokes with a birdie on eleven. We've never vetoed a bill, but we've volleyed a ball; we've never faced a full press corps, but we've faced a full-court press. The politics, in the end, are subjective; sports are objective.

A presidential foul shot is taken from the same distance as you would from the charity stripe on your driveway. A pitch from a major league mound is 60'6" for both you and the leader of the free world. The distance to run a marathon is the same for a person who won the Electoral College as it is for someone who never went to college.

In our never-ending quest to quantify, qualify, list and rank everything in the known universe, our best and brightest stat geeks have thus far ignored the athletic accomplishments of our commanders-in-chief — despite an enormous amount of mainstream interest in the athletic skills of our presidents.

If our most recent presidents have taught us anything — whether it's golf pundits keeping track of President Trump's handicap, or ESPN airing a special about President Obama's pick-up basketball games, or photographers following President Bush as he mountain bikes through Beijing during the Olympics, or cameras tracking President Clinton as he jogs through Washington, D.C. — it's that when they engage in physical activity, the media will follow.

And this isn't just a modern phenomenon. Photographers used to camp out on the White House grass to catch Eisenhower practicing his short irons on the south lawn. The grainy home video of the Kennedy family tossing around a football at Camelot is practically ingrained in our public consciousness. The same can be said for ceremonial first pitches from William Howard Taft, Woodrow Wilson or Richard Nixon; or charity tennis matches with Jimmy Carter and George H.W. Bush; or shots of Gerald Ford swimming laps in the outdoor pool he installed at the White House. Even George Washington performed a feat of strength at Mt. Vernon for a member of the "media."

We've been obsessed with our presidents as athletes for as long as there have been presidents and athletes.

Which president saved 77 lives during his time as a lifeguard? Which president's lucky handball is still sitting in the Smithsonian more than a century after he last played with it? Which president invented a sport? Which one practiced jiu-jitsu three afternoons a week while in office? Or was an NCAA champion? The answers to these questions (Reagan, Lincoln, Hoover, Teddy Roosevelt and Ford, respectively) barely scratch the surface of the athletic information available on our presidents, which is why I harnessed the power of statistics and the spirit of sabermetrics to create a system and properly crown one of our presidents as king of the executive athletic arena.

Jocks in Chief is the first ever comprehensive ranking of the athletic abilities of every United States president, using an entirely transparent, sabermetrics style ratings system to establish a top 10 and ultimately a clear winner.

With that in mind, I wrote a short to long-ish essay on each president's athletic career, taking into account the different eras and how certain athletic skills were perceived at the time. For instance, during the first hundred years of our nation, a man's ability to ride a horse was directly related to how he was perceived as an athlete.

After writing each essay, I ranked every president according to his White House Athlete Ranking, or WhAR (I'll explain below), and I included my justification for each score.

The WhAR (White House Athlete Ranking)

The foundation of this book is something I invented called the WhAR. Much in the same way Mel Kiper Jr. breaks down the individual talents of college football players before the NFL draft, I have analyzed the specific talents of our presidents and assigned them a number (1-10) in each of the following categories to come up with their score:

Executive Power — ranks a president's overall physical strength

This could be earned in the weight room, in battle, on the field or through feats of strength during their lives. It even takes into account "big guy" strength for some of our larger office holders.

Running Ability — ranks a president's physical fitness and cardio throughout their lives (both before and after office)

Since presidents typically take office a few decades after their prime years as an athlete, this category was included to focus on a president's prime and athletic achievements *prior* to taking office (or even after, in some cases). Factors that are considered here are regular exercise routines or pick-up sports, being a member of a college or high school team, or any lifelong athletic hobbies a president may have.

Fit for Office — ranks how fit a president stayed once in office

To properly score a president's athletic ability, I thought it would be important to include a separate category for their athleticism while in the White House. This includes any physical activity or daily fitness habits that a president performed *during their term* as POTUS.

Executive Experience — ranks the athletic accomplishments of a president

This category deals with concrete athletic achievements by a president during their lifetime — their true résumé as an athlete, if you will. It will include any individual or team records a president has set, championships they won or scholarships they earned. It also includes notable performances or accomplishments such as running a marathon or biking a hard trail, playing on a high-level varsity squad in high school or college (or the pros) and things along those lines.

Mettle of Honor — ranks a president's athletic toughness and endurance

This is a bit of a catch-all category designed to even out the eras in terms of what could be considered a "gritty performance." In addition to accomplishments like running a marathon, which is tough to do, we have presidents who have walked 100 miles straight, presidents who have fought through bullet wounds en route to winning battles, presidents who swam miles in the ocean while dragging fellow sailors to safety, presidents who rescued dozens of people as a lifeguard, and a president who was an offensive lineman on the football field. This category takes into account all those things and more.

Using these numbers as a guide, I've divided this book into two parts: **Off the Ballot** and **The Contenders**.

Part I: Off the Ballot

The first part of this book features the presidents that fall in the bottom half of the rankings, and I have divided them into three chapters: **Commanders in Beef**, **The Van Buren Boys**, and **Lame Ducks**. These are not indicative of their exact WhAR order, but rather a way to group them in the category that makes the most sense.

Part II: The Contenders

This section will feature the presidents who land in the top half of the rankings, and will culminate in the revealing of our most athletic president. This section will be divided into four chapters: **White House Weekend Warriors, National Treasures, Sultans of the Smithsonian** and **Mount Rushmore — The Athletes.**

And with that, let's begin...

Part I: Off the Ballot

While the following men were picked by the American people to lead as president, they likely would have been among the last picked by their classmates on the playground. Some were too small, some were too fat, others were too dainty (I'm looking at you, James Buchanan), but all were simply better equipped for the political arena than the athletic arena.

As baseball has the Mendoza line to signify hitting futility, these presidents have the Madison line. Since none of the following are contenders for the title of Most Athletic President, I've grouped them into categories that unite them otherwise, putting aside their sheer athletic futility.

Keep in mind that the highest total WhAR a president can score is 50. The lowest is 5.

CHAPTER 1:
COMMANDERS IN BEEF

Some presidents were larger than life. These presidents were just large.

William Howard Taft

HEIGHT: 6'
WEIGHT: 340 (at his peak)
COLLEGE: Yale
SPORTS: General Exercise, Walking, Golf

A QUICK ANECDOTE about William Howard Taft's tremendous size: President Taft often visited his summer home in Beverly Bay, Massachusetts, and on one particularly beautiful New England morning he put on his trunks and decided to go for a swim. A neighbor, watching Taft in the waves, suggested to another resident that they should dive in as well. "Better wait," the second man said. "The President is using the ocean."

Ba-dum tss!

While Taft wasn't the first president to be mocked for his physical appearance (wait until you hear the nicknames people had for John Adams), he did set a presidential precedent when it came to the press corps' interest in his size and his efforts to slim down. Considering his enormous 54-inch waist, rumors that he got stuck in the White House bathtub (true) and his nickname "Big Lub," Taft stands alone as the most obese man to ever occupy the Oval Office.

What people may not realize, however, is that Big Lub did everything he could to fight the fat. A *New York Times* article from July 11, 1910 titled "Taft Working to Reduce — President Boxes and Wrestles, and Hopes to Take Off 25 Pounds," describes Taft's workout regimen as he attempted to lose the weight. It included daily 7 a.m. sessions with his trainer Dr. Charles E. Barker. The reason for the sessions, as the article kindly put it, was because "during the winter he [Taft] has been so busy that his exercise has been omitted and he has accumulated a large quantity of additional tissue."

Additional tissue (otherwise known as "fat" to the rest of us) would plague Taft for much of his 63 years on Earth. However, to portray the 27th president as a slob or someone who didn't care about his health would be wildly unfair. Taft valiantly fought his metabolism and genetics, and enlisted the help of British dietitian Nathaniel Edward-Yorke Davis, a sort of Richard Simmons of his time, to create a weight-loss program for him.

For the better part of two decades, Taft recorded all of his meals, workouts and other physical activity in a journal as a way to track and tame his ever-expanding belly. Throughout his time as Secretary of War, as president, and then during Act III of his career as the 10th Chief Justice of the Supreme Court (yes, he had one of the most storied political careers in U.S. history) he experimented with exercise habits, eventually finding one that he stuck to.

During his tenure as chief justice, he walked six miles round trip from his home to the Capitol every day. In fact, he often took Connecticut Avenue on his route home and used a small crossing over Rock Creek, which was renamed the Taft Bridge after his death. In 1929 — the year before he died — he had lost more than 100 pounds from his peak weight and clocked in at 244 pounds (although his illness contributed to some of his weight loss).

WhAR (White House Athlete Ranking)

Executive Power

While Taft wasn't exactly benching 300 pounds and squatting 500 while in the Oval Office, he was a big man all of his life and had what we'd now call "natural strength" as opposed to gym strength. Case in point, he was once an intramural heavyweight wrestling champion in high school. As such, Taft would surely mop the floor with some of our smaller, meeker presidents, putting him in the middle of the power pack.

SCORE: 5

Running Ability

We covered the extent to which Taft tried to keep himself in shape while in office, and though valiant efforts were made, there will be no pity points here. He still spent much of his pre-POTUS life at well over 300 pounds, and for that reason his fitness points stay near the bottom.

SCORE: 3

Fit for Office

Whereas the previous category ranks the president's ability to stay fit over the course of his life, this category ranks his general fitness and athletic ability while in office. The results again speak for themselves, however, Taft certainly gets points here for effort.

SCORE: 4

Executive Achievement

There were presidents who ran marathons, played on NCAA championship teams, earned college scholarships, and even had offers to play in the pros. Taft had none of these. But his aforementioned wrestling skills do count for something, as does his commitment to daily six-mile walks while in his 50s.

SCORE: 3

Mettle of Honor:

The scores in this category are reserved for feats of strength, courage shown in battle and/or physical achievements that required toughness, grit and gumption. Not much to report here for Taft, other than the war against his waistline.

SCORE: 3

WhAR: 18

Overall Ranking: #25

Warren G. Harding

HEIGHT: 6'
WEIGHT: 240
COLLEGE: Ohio Central College
SPORTS: Poker

WHILE WARREN G. Harding's 6-foot, 240-pound frame suggests a stout middle linebacker or fullback, the fact is that Harding was actually more of a *Soft*ing (*a-thank you very much*). As a young man, "Wobbly Warren" suffered from exhaustion and nervous fatigue so many times that he often landed in the Battle Creek Sanitarium to regain his health. In an effort to find some scrap of athletic achievement in Harding's history, we're forced to count one of his favorite pastimes, poker, as a sport. There's little chance, however, that our 29th president would have landed in the World Series of Poker, as his most famous card story involves wagering and losing a set of White House china in a game of no-limit Texas Hold 'Em. Apparently, no-limit even includes dinnerware owned by the people of the United States.

The interesting thing about Warren G. (which stands for Gamaliel), is that he was actually very popular during his lifetime. But after his untimely death at the age of 57, a series of scandals and affairs were revealed, and rocked his legacy to the point that he is often ranked last or near last on most lists of greatest presidents.

In an effort to uncover some fortitude, I took into account that he grew up in rural Ohio, which means he had to have some level of toughness — but there is scant record of any type of physical pursuits. He did own several newspapers as a young man, but hitting deadlines is a far cry from hitting baseballs. If you're thinking that Harding was born during a period when sports weren't a big deal, you'd be wrong. He took office just as Babe Ruth was taking over the outfield for the New York Yankees, so this isn't a case of sports not being a "thing" while Harding was in office. It's more a case of Harding not being into sports as a kid, as a politician or as president.

However (and this is a stretch) the high school in Warren, Ohio that is named for President Harding (Warren G. Harding High School) won a state baseball championship in 1933, two football championships in the 1970s, one football title in the '90s, and a track and field title in 2010. Several former NFL players attended the school, including Mario Manningham and Ross Browner, as well as Hall of Fame wide receiver Paul Warfield.

None of this reflects on Harding's actual athletic ability, but his name is at least tangentially associated with sports excellence.

WhAR (White House Athlete Ranking)

Executive Power

I've decided to give Harding a power score in the middle of the pack for a similar reason as I did Taft. He didn't necessarily display any athletic prowess, but he was a large man, and simple common sense says he'd be much stronger than some of the smaller guys like James Madison who rose to the presidency.

SCORE: 3.5

Running Ability

Nope.

SCORE: 1

Fit for Office

There is nothing to report. Sorry, Warren.

SCORE: 1

Executive Achievement

Marathon poker games are impressive, but they get you no points on this list. Actual marathons, as you'll see later, certainly weigh heavily.

SCORE: 1

Mettle of Honor:

Harding likely suffered from a heart condition most of his life, so his lack of accomplishments here aren't entirely his fault. Still, it's hard to give points for toughness and grit as an athlete when he never competed in anything that didn't involve a deck of cards.

SCORE: 1

WhAR: 7.5

OVERALL RANKING: #39

Grover Cleveland

HEIGHT: 5'11"
WEIGHT: 250
COLLEGE: none
SPORTS: Hunting, Fishing, Drinking, Poker

CLEVELAND LIVED IN a time when toughness, endurance and fitness were measured on the battlefield. Unfortunately, we can't measure him by any of these things. Although he was drafted to serve in the Civil War, he took advantage of the Conscription Act, which allowed him to pay someone to serve in his place. That someone was a Polish immigrant named George Benninsky, who received $150 for his troubles (roughly $3,000 in today's money).

With no wartime, athletic or fitness endeavors under his belt, Cleveland tipped the scales at well over 250 pounds while he was in office (spanning both of his non-consecutive terms), making him the clear second-place finisher to Taft in the most-out-of-shape-president department.

Unlike Taft, however, Cleveland was *not* obsessed with trying to lose weight. He was known to have a voracious appetite for both food and drink, and even his minor attempts to curb the latter habit fell flat. One famous story involving Cleveland and his love of alcohol took place during his 1870 campaign for district attorney of Erie County, New York. While on the campaign trail, he and his rival agreed to limit their beer consumption to four glasses a day, which seemed reasonable to both of them — at least for a little while. After a relatively short amount of time, Cleveland decided that anything less than a six-pack a day wouldn't cut it, so he bailed on the plan.

To nobody's surprise, the constant swilling of beer steadily increased his waistline to the point that he had earned the nickname

"Uncle Jumbo" by the time he finally won the presidency. Funny enough, this was actually the second girth-related nickname he had acquired in his life. While most people knew him as "Grover," his real first name was Steve, and those who knew him well often referred to him as "Big Steve."

And as you might expect, a guy called Big Steve was a man's man. He smoked cigars. He liked to hunt. He enjoyed fishing. He loved poker — all excellent traits for a drinking buddy, not a teammate in pick-up hoops.

WhAR (White House Athlete Ranking)

Executive Power

Uncle Jumbo gets the obligatory "big guy" points in the strength department, but that's about it. Twelve-ounce curls don't really count here.

SCORE: 5

Running Ability

Um. No.

SCORE: 1

Fit for Office

Nope.

SCORE: 1

Executive Achievement

It's actually amazing that after two terms in office served over 12 years there is so little to report here.

SCORE: 1

Mettle of Honor:

When it comes to the courage department, paying someone to serve in a war for you doesn't even qualify you for a score of 1, so we're going to give Cleveland the very rare, but well-earned, goose egg.

SCORE: 0

WhAR: 8

OVERALL RANKING: #38

Chester A. Arthur

HEIGHT: 6'2"
WEIGHT: 220
COLLEGE: Union College
SPORTS: Walking

IN A 2009 article, *Time* magazine listed Chester A. Arthur as one of the most forgettable presidents we've ever had — a designation that also applies to his athletic abilities and achievements. Actually, that's not entirely accurate. To *forget* an achievement implies that one actually took place. After much digging, only a single instance of regular physical exertion comes to the forefront for Arthur, and it involves walking.

"Chet," as his pals called him, was one of five presidents to take office without being elected (he ascended to the presidency after James Garfield was assassinated), and he had a rough go of it once he began his administration. His cabinet was filled with enemies, and the Republicans who helped him get the vice presidency turned on him and he became incredibly stressed out. To alleviate the tension, Arthur often went for hour-long walks at 2 a.m.

And that's the story of why he walked.

Physically, he was a husky guy at 6-foot-2 and 220 pounds, and he did serve in the military during the Civil War as a brigadier general, but he never saw combat. He was an efficient organizer of men, and despite several opportunities to lead troops into battle his superiors asked him to stay behind the front lines to oversee the logistics of the troops.

When it came to ranking presidents athletically, Arthur was one of the hardest to pin down. Every time I'd uncover a fact that looked like it might lead to some shred of athleticism, I was thwarted. For instance, I found out that he was called the "Dude

President," and I thought that surely this will take me down the path to some cool "dude" achievement. Alas, "dude" in the time of Chester A. Arthur referred to a man who was interested in fashion (who knew?). Apparently, he had a well-known affinity for wearing things like high hats, frock coats and silken scarves — so much so that he was also dubbed the "Gentleman Boss" and "Elegant Arthur," two names that have nothing to do with fitness or sports.

It's too bad this book doesn't rank the fashionistas in chief, because Arthur once reportedly tried on 20 pairs of pants to find the right fit. If only that kind of dedication was given to tailoring his physique instead of fitting in time with his tailor, he'd have earned a higher WhAR score.

WhAR (White House Athlete Ranking)

Executive Power
Standing 6-foot-2 and weighing well over 200 pounds puts Chet near the top of our presidents in terms of size, so the "size equals power" rule applies here and he gets a nominal bump.

SCORE: 5

Running Ability
Walking isn't running.

SCORE: 3

Fit for Office
Nada.

SCORE: 1

Executive Achievement

As with any fitness routine, something is better than nothing, so we've got to give Arthur credit for his nightly hour-long walks.

SCORE: 2

Mettle of Honor:

Serving in a war in any capacity, even if he never saw battle, has to give Arthur a point over the presidents who never served or competed in any athletic endeavors. It's a stretch, for sure, but it's something.

SCORE: 3

WhAR: 14

OVERALL RANKING: #32

John Adams

HEIGHT: 5'7"
WEIGHT: 170 (estimated)
COLLEGE: Harvard
SPORTS: Hunting, Fishing, Walking

IN A LETTER to his son Charles, John Adams wrote, "Move or die is the language of our Maker in the constitution of our bodies." That's not exactly "Just Do It" for the 18th century, but it's a better exercise philosophy than most, and one that Adams took to heart — at least in terms of getting outside and away from his desk.

While never a soldier or an outdoorsman, Adams routinely rose at 5 a.m. and made it a point to take a long walk every day. During his time in France negotiating on behalf of the American colonies (and living with his roommate Ben Franklin) Adams walked five or six miles every day through the Bois de Boulogne, often bringing his son and future president John Quincy with him. But despite his love of a good stroll and the occasional fishing or hunting trip, Adams simply was not an athlete. Even as a teenager, he was short and what we'd politely call "stout," and he never outgrew his sensitivity to comments about his appearance or physique.

Later in life he was asked to describe what he looked like, and through clenched teeth he said, "I have one head, four limbs and five senses, like any other man, and nothing peculiar in any of them ... I have no miniature and have been too much abused by painters ever to sit to anyone again."

Since painters are slightly less accurate than selfies, we'll take Adams' word for it that the wide variety of portraits of him, though consistent across canvases and time periods, weren't exactly flattering. But artists weren't the only ones who were seemingly taking shots at him. Even his fellow politicians had a knack for getting under his skin for all the extra flesh under his skin.

Behind his back, rivals — and members of his own party — referred to him with an all-time nickname that managed to capture both sarcasm and the absurd pomp and circumstance that came with official government titles in the late 1700s, dubbing him: His Rotundity.

One habit that no doubt helped him maintain his rotundity was his morning ritual of drinking hard cider with breakfast, a habit he picked up in college and seemingly only broke while in Philadelphia at the Constitutional Convention. But if you're thinking he broke the habit because he decided to forego the cider in favor of coffee or water or tea while forming a new nation, you'd be wrong. He only bailed on his beloved drink because he fell in love with something else even more: Philly brewskies.

In a letter to his wife Abigail, quoted in David McCullough's brilliant book *John Adams* (where much of this information came from), Adams wrote, "I drink no cider, but feast on Philadelphia beer."

Despite his lack of athletic hobbies outside of walking, and a breakfast of beer or cider for most of his life (along with bacon and cheese and biscuits), Adams lived to be 90 years old, an astonishing feat during a time when most men just hoped to reach their 50s. Rotund or not, if the point of exercising and eating healthy is to increase longevity, Adams was doing something right. Here's to hard cider for breakfast tomorrow morning!

WhAR (White House Athlete Ranking)

Executive Power

As we've discussed, Adams was short and portly and had neither the size nor the necessary physical activities to scrape together a decent score in this category.

SCORE: 2

Running Ability

To the extent that walking or strolling gets any credit, the length of Adams' walks and the lifelong consistency bump him up a half-point higher than other POTUSes who also claim walking as their sole athletic skill.

SCORE: 2.5

Fit for Office

Again, walking.

SCORE: 1

Executive Achievement

Are we still talking about taking regular long walks?

SCORE: 1

Mettle of Honor:

Adams didn't serve as a soldier in the Revolutionary War, but by signing the Declaration of Independence he was essentially signing a death warrant should the British win or catch him and try him for treason. For that reason, we have to give Adams a solid 3 for toughness here.

SCORE: 3

WhAR: 9.5

OVERALL RANKING: #35

Bill Clinton

HEIGHT: 6'2"
WEIGHT: 230
COLLEGE: Yale
SPORTS: Jogging, Golf

"I WAS A fat band boy" is not a quote you would expect to hear from a great athlete; it's a quote you would hear from a man who knows his physical limitations. In the case of President Bill Clinton, those limitations were pronounced. Clinton's battles with his waistline were famously played out in the media during his presidency, often leading to easy jokes on the late-night shows. The most famous of those jokes was the *Saturday Night Live* skit in which Phil Hartman (playing Clinton) jogged his way to a McDonald's. Under the guise of "talking with some real folks and maybe getting a diet Coke or something," he ends up eating the customers' food and asking the manager to make an Egg McMuffin with extra sausages just for him — to which he later adds barbecue sauce. He then proceeds to take a bite of nearly everything on the menu.

So, yes, Clinton's weight and love for fast food were very much an issue during his time in office. In addition to his thrice-weekly jog of exactly 27 minutes (three, eight-minute miles and change, according to a Secret Service agent), Clinton also played golf regularly. As is the custom with Commanders-in-Chief, he often found himself on the course with legendary athletes, one instance of which led to what may be the most impressive athletic moment of his life: the time he hit a drive farther than 18-time major winner Jack Nicklaus.

This is how he described it on ESPN's *Mike and Mike* radio show:

"We played this one par-5 hole and I outdrove Jack Nicklaus

by a foot," Clinton said. "He looks at me and I could tell he didn't like it. We were both on this par-5 green in two [shots], and I was only eight feet away from an eagle. I had never had an eagle on a par-5 hole. Ever. And I literally stubbed the putt. It was the worst putt you could have imagined. Jack Nicklaus looked at me and said, 'You didn't think you were worthy of an eagle, did you?' I said, 'I guess not.' He smiled and he said, 'You need to get over that.' I'll never forget that for as long as I live."

Aside from outdriving the Golden Bear, Clinton's self-professed second-best athletic moment came in a church league pick-up basketball game, when he scored 16 points and almost dunked the ball. Both his one-night scoring prowess and the near-dunk in the game were surprises — even to him.

In the same interview with *Mike & Mike* in which he talked about his once-in-a-lifetime drive, he discusses his one shining moment thusly:

"I was in a church league. I wasn't very good, I was too heavy. But I would run pretty well in short distances. One night I was the leading scorer on our team. I scored 16 points in a church league game, never have before or since," he said. "And I nearly dunked a ball! And I was only, at the time, 6 feet tall. I don't know what happened. It was just one of those magical nights. My hand got like right at the rim and I almost got the ball dunked in. I figured maybe every human being on Earth is granted one good day in a sports game."

While the almost-dunking story doesn't overshadow him dunking untold McNuggets into Sweet and Sour sauce, it does give us a glimpse into President Clinton's peak athletic skill, which comes in handy as we tally our WhAR score.

WhAR (White House Athlete Ranking)

Executive Power

Standing at 6-foot-2 and weighing roughly 220 to 230 pounds, Bubba, as Clinton was nicknamed, was not a small man. He didn't lift weights and he didn't play any physical sports, but outdriving the greatest golfer of all time, even once, has to be worth something in the power department.

SCORE: 5

Running Ability

Bill Clinton wasn't the marathon runner and mountain biker his successor George W. Bush was, and he wasn't nearly the athlete of the man who held the office before him, George H.W. Bush, but jogging three times a week is better than nothing and gets him out of the basement for this category.

SCORE: 2

Fit for Office

The difference between the Running Ability and Fit for Office categories is that the former ranks a president's physical fitness and cardio throughout his life, and the latter ranks it according to what he did in office. As we've seen, other than jogging and golf, Clinton didn't work out much. And while he occasionally lost weight (only to gain it back), his time in the White House is largely one where he maintained a husky frame.

SCORE: 2

Executive Achievement

Almost dunking a basketball does not count as an athletic achievement. Nor does a single-double in a church league basketball game. Hitting a better drive than Jack Nicklaus is just enough to put Clinton out of the dreaded 1 category and place him in the 2s.

SCORE: 2

Mettle of Honor:

This category is a measure of endurance and courage and grit. Golfing and jogging don't exactly test any of those three things, and Clinton had no military service to lean on here either. Alas, he earns himself a 1.

SCORE: 1

WhAR: 12

OVERALL RANKING: #30

CHAPTER 2:
THE VAN BUREN BOYS

While all presidents promise to uphold the Bill of Rights, this elevation-challenged group could have used a Bill of Heights.

James Madison

HEIGHT: 5'4"
WEIGHT: 100 (estimated)
COLLEGE: Princeton
SPORTS: None

THE SHORTEST PRESIDENT in U.S. history was a contemporary of Napoleon, so it's doubtful he had the complex named after the European leader. However, his short stature was such that Washington Irving described him at his presidential inauguration as being "but a withered little apple-John." Not exactly an image that evokes great physical ability. To be fair to Madison, he was sick for most of his childhood and suffered from stress-induced seizures until he was a young adult. He had a soaring intellect that allowed him to write the U.S. Constitution, become President, graduate Princeton in two years, and master Greek, Latin and Hebrew. Brain power: yes. Athletic ability: none whatsoever

Unlike some of our other less physically gifted presidents, Madison didn't even have the habit of a daily stroll to lean on. He rode his horse around his plantation in Montpelier when he was home, and in the book *James Madison: A Biography,* author Ralph Ketcham explains that some days he didn't go on the horse ride and instead raced his wife Dolley around their giant porch. But even if that qualified as a workout (it doesn't), Madison wasn't going to be wolfing down protein shakes and drinking water to rehydrate. He was a whiskey man through and through, reportedly drinking about a pint of the hard stuff a day.

On a personal note, I attended James Madison University in Harrisonburg, Virginia. While Madison seemingly didn't have a shred of athleticism in his tiny body, it is worth nothing that when it comes to his sports legacy, the school named after him is doing an admirable job of linking his name to excellence on the field.

The football team has won two national championships (2004, 2016), the field hockey team won one (1994), and so did the women's lacrosse team (2018). The school also produced NFL Hall of Famer and five-time Super Bowl champion Charles Haley as well as Pro Bowl wide receiver Gary Clark.

Yes, roping in athletes and accomplishments that were won for a school that bears a president's name is absolutely a stretch and has nothing whatsoever to do with Madison's own athletic ability, but when it comes to our fourth president that's all we can really do. If we wanted to stretch things even further, we could include the University of Wisconsin's accomplishments on the field of play, which would add 18 men's and seven women's titles to the mix, including six ice hockey and five cross country rings. Why Wisconsin? Because the university is based in Madison, a town named after, you guessed it, James Madison.

And thus ends our extreme detour to find even a scintilla of sports skill to tie to Madison, who is truly one of the very few presidents to have zero athletic, military or even physical accomplishments to his name.

WhAR (White House Athlete Ranking)

Executive Power
Nope.

SCORE: 1

Running Ability
No.

SCORE: 1

Fit For Office

Nada.

SCORE: 1

Executive Achievement

Zip.

SCORE: 1

Mettle of Honor:

Madison gets the standard 3 here for putting his life on the line while he wrote the new Constitution and served as a massively important founding father while under the threat of death if caught by the British.

SCORE: 3

WhAR: 7

OVERALL RANKING: #40

Martin Van Buren

HEIGHT: 5'6"
WEIGHT: 160 (estimated)
COLLEGE: None
SPORTS: Horse Riding

MARTIN VAN BUREN was a forgettable president with an unexceptional résumé both physically and politically. Prior to his presidency, he was briefly governor of New York, and served as secretary of state and vice president for Andrew Jackson before winning the presidency after Jackson left office. Four years later, he was unceremoniously voted out, and historians have lumped him in with the other ineffective one-term presidents of his era.

Van Buren had no daily exercise habits, no military experience, and no physical hobbies. Even as a child, his nickname of Little Mat connotes a lack of size and strength. As an adult, Van Buren was short, stout and suffered from asthma. There are almost no records of him even breaking a sweat, let alone exercising. In an era of "No Name Presidents," MVB was certainly not a contender for MVP of the Oval Office. I'm sorry there isn't more, but there simply isn't.

I can offer you this piece of information, however, courtesy of potus.com:

"The term 'O.K.' was popularized because of Van Buren. Van Buren was from Kinderhook, New York, sometimes referred to as Old Kinderhook in speeches and print. O.K. Clubs soon formed to support Van Buren's campaign. 'O.K.' later came to mean 'all right.'"

O.K.?

I know, I know. There should be more about a president's physical achievements, but there just isn't. I've flipped through the only real biography of Van Buren, written by historian Ted Widmer, but came up empty. I spent time on the digital home of his presidential historical site, and it's completely devoid of anything resembling a sport or exercise.

One thing that is always mentioned in relation to Van Buren is his ludicrous hair, which is part Bozo the Clown and part blow-dried sideburns sideshow. According to the Official Martin Van Buren Sideburns Appreciation Society (yes, it's a real site: **www. joshgulch.com**) Van Buren's "*Massive vibrissae would often offer safe harbor for birds, squirrels and the occasional stray cat seeking refuge from the cold.*"

Clearly we've veered off topic here, but with a total absence of athleticism, I thought I'd at least add to your Van Buren knowledge beyond what you learned from Kramer and the Van Buren Boys on *Seinfeld*.

WhAR (White House Athlete Ranking)

Executive Power

No.

SCORE: 1

Running Ability

Nope.

SCORE: 1

Fit For Office

To illustrate how little Van Buren valued exercise, John Quincy Adams once visited Van Buren at the White House in 1839, later writing this little gem in his diary: "Mr. Van Buren is growing inordinately fat."

SCORE: 1

Executive Achievement

Uh-uh.

SCORE: 1

Mettle of Honor:

Sorry, Little Mat.

SCORE: 1.5

WhAR: 5.5

OVERALL RANKING: #43

James K. Polk

HEIGHT: 5'8"
WEIGHT: 140
COLLEGE: University of North Carolina
SPORTS: None

JAMES K. POLK could have attended the University of North Carolina (his alma mater) at the same time as Michael Jordan, and there's a good chance they would have never met. MJ wasn't a regular at the debate club or the math club, and it appears that Polk may have had an allergy to physical activity. Growing up in Tennessee, he spent most of his childhood between illnesses, culminating in having gall stones removed when he was only 16 years old.

Even on his official president website, **JamesKPolk.com**, they take a quick dig at how fragile he was, writing, "Although young Polk was accustomed to the rigors of frontier life, he lacked physical stamina."

Ouch.

Polk overcompensated for his lack of physical ability by being a workaholic, often burying himself in his studies or work for days at a time. In fact, while in the Oval Office, Polk famously said, "No president who performs his duties faithfully and conscientiously can have any leisure."

Nearly every president in this book would disagree and look to engage in some sort of leisurely activity. Polk, on the other hand, worked himself to the bone while he was president, and with no healthy habits or exercises built into his schedule he had no way to relieve stress, blow off steam or otherwise counteract the pressures of his job.

During his campaign for the presidency, Polk made a promise

to serve only one term, and as it turned out that was just about all he could handle. The strain of the job was so great that when his term was up, he honored his pledge and chose to not run again. Publicly, he claimed he was honoring his promise and that he had accomplished his major goals while in office, the most important of which was the western expansion of the United States to the Pacific Ocean. Privately, his mind and his body were exhausted. Although he entered office at the age of 49, making him the youngest president at the time, the four years he worked in the White House sucked the life out of him and he left the Capitol in poor health.

Three months after his presidency ended, he died of cholera like a poor sap in the Oregon Trail video game.

WhAR (White House Athlete Ranking)

Executive Power

The words "strength" and "Polk" don't often collide in the same sentence when reading about our 11th president. After extensive research, there is no evidence that he ever exerted himself physically outside of picking up stacks of books.

SCORE: 1

Running Ability

Usually we'd give Polk a few points here for surviving on the frontier as a young man, but from what we've read, he was barely able to do that.

SCORE: 1

Fit for Office

Polk's quote about having zero time for leisure activity — including exercise or sports — keeps him at the bottom of the barrel for this category.

SCORE: 1

Executive Achievement

When it comes to any kind of athletic accomplishment, we *polked* around (sorry, had to) and found nothing. Sorry, James.

SCORE: 1

Mettle of Honor:

Polk may have been known as the "Napoleon of debate," but when it comes to physical toughness and courage, it seems he had about as much grit as a tub of Napoleon ice cream.

SCORE: 1

WhAR: 5

OVERALL RANKING: #44

Millard Fillmore

HEIGHT: 5'9"
WEIGHT: 160
COLLEGE: none
SPORTS: Walking

WHETHER OR NOT you consider long-distance walking a sport will determine where you place Millard Fillmore in the bottom section of these rankings. If you think endurance walking should count toward his WhAR score, then Fillmore's one "athletic" achievement is quite impressive. If not, he languishes with the other non-athletes in presidential purgatory. Here's the feat and the story behind it:

When Millard Fillmore was a young man, his father arranged a clothing apprenticeship for him that was tantamount to slavery. He was basically "sold" to a factory and forced to work ungodly hours for extremely little pay and no time to go to school or even learn to read. As you can imagine, young Millard was miserable and dreamed of getting out.

After suffering long enough, the future president went around town begging for money, finally scraping together 30 dollars to buy his freedom. Also, this took place in the dead of winter in upstate New York. Upon purchasing his freedom, he couldn't exactly call an Uber to take him home, which was more than 100 miles away. So… Fillmore put one foot in front of the other and walked. The. Whole. Way.

As the story goes, he didn't stop once the entire way, suffering the cold and wind and hunger — all in a quest to get back to the dad who had sold him away in the first place. When you're scraping the bottom of the barrel for athletic achievements, this marathon walk has to count for something. After all, if you do that trek in Alaska, you at least get a bunch of sled dogs to help.

The reason I spent so much time on this story is because it is both fascinating and impressive — and it's the only information on Fillmore I could find that includes an activity that could be categorized as fitness.

He was a lawyer by trade, didn't serve in the military, and didn't hunt or fish or participate in any outdoor activities that would constitute athleticism. Also, Fillmore only took over for Old Rough and Ready President Taylor after he passed away, leaving us with a shortened term to evaluate his in-office habits. Overall, Fillmore was smack dab in the middle of the list of forgettable presidents, and we have no choice but to include his lack of athletic aptitude in that category as well.

WhAR (White House Athlete Ranking)

Executive Power

We have no evidence of exceptional strength or power, and with his average size there's no reason to assume any.

SCORE: 2

Running Ability

Eh. This one is hard to judge as well. We have nothing to work off. He wasn't obese, so he at least took care of himself enough to stay thin-ish. That has to count for something.

SCORE: 2

Fit for Office

Fillmore served for roughly three years after President Taylor's death, and there is little record of his daily habits or exercise.

SCORE: 2

Executive Achievement

This is where that "100-mile walk in the dead of winter" story can score Fillmore some much-needed WhAR points. It's not exactly a true athletic endeavor, but it is…something.

SCORE: 2.5

Mettle of Honor:

Again, we're relying on one signature feat to measure his toughness. The Walk. I'm willing to give him a hard 6 for this.

SCORE: 6

WhAR: 14.5

OVERALL RANKING: #31

Benjamin Harrison

HEIGHT: 5'6"
WEIGHT: 140
COLLEGE: Miami (Ohio)
SPORTS: none

JAMES MADISON WAS short, but his nickname was at least a positive one: "The Great Little Madison." Benjamin Harrison, who was the second-shortest president ever to serve, was simply known as "Little Ben" — not even "Mediocre Little Ben" or "The Average Little Harrison." Harrison grew up a farmer, spending his days outside tending cattle, hauling wood, hunting and fishing. He served in a voluntary military regiment during the Civil War and was honored by Abraham Lincoln.

When researching stories about Harrison's athletic ability and/or feats, one that stands out involves Harrison's pet goat Old Whiskers, who spent much of his time pulling Harrison's grandchildren around the White House grounds on a small cart. One day, Old Whiskers evidently had had enough of the Harrison grandkids and made a run for it, dashing through an open gate and breaking out of the White House — with Harrison's grandchildren still in tow.

President Harrison happened to be waiting for his own carriage in front of the White House when the goat took off. Realizing his grandkids could be in danger, Harrison ran after the little entourage, waving his cane and using his other hand to hold on to his top hat. Thankfully, the goat ran out of steam after only a few blocks, but not before D.C. residents were treated to the sight of their Commander-In-Chief huffing and puffing down the street after a goat.

Is this an athletic achievement?

Well, it's not *not* an athletic achievement. And it's the only thing I uncovered in terms of Harrison breaking a sweat during his term in office. It was known that he liked to walk, fly fish and hunt, but there wasn't any evidence I could find of workouts or participation in sports. In terms of what he was like as a politician, I did find this gem of a quote from Teddy Roosevelt, who called him a "cold-blooded, narrow-minded, prejudiced, obstinate, timid old psalm-singing Indianapolis politician."

Suffice to say, it doesn't sound like the notoriously fit TR was inviting "Little Ben" over for any wrestling or sparring sessions.

Something interesting I did notice during a quick photo tour of Harrison's personal house was that he kept a workout chest filled with clubs, a few sets of dumbbells, cables and other various exercise equipment. I reached out to the Benjamin Harrison presidential site to inquire about Harrison's exercise, as well as his home gym, and Jennifer Capps, the vice president of curatorship and exhibition wrote me this response:

"I do not think Benjamin Harrison had any 'training' schedule. We did not know how much he may or may not have used the Whitney Home Gymnasium that is in our collection. It is an original Harrison artifact (it belonged to him) and even shows up at the White House during his administration."

Capps also shared a story regarding one of Mrs. Harrison's daughters allegedly trying to use the gym. She said, *"Indeed I did, I remember one time pulling too hard and it all came down on top of me."*

Capps surmised that if the girl could pull it over, it wasn't attached to the wall as it should have been for regular use, which means Harrison most likely didn't use it regularly (although this would have been towards the end of his life when this story took place.)

WhAR (White House Athlete Ranking)

Executive Power

As I stated, Harrison was a small guy, and power moves outside of politics were not really his bag. But he had a home gym, which has to count for something.

SCORE: 2

Running Ability

Harrison was thin and kept himself so his whole life. This may have been the result of a strong metabolism or a small appetite (or anything other than physical activity), but whatever the reason, remaining svelte has to count for something. It's not like he was too out of shape to chase down his grandkids in a goat-cart (C'mon… goat cart? That got you. Admit it.)

SCORE: 1

Fit for Office

We have no evidence that Harrison performed any physical activity or exercise while in office.

SCORE: 1.5

Executive Achievement

Let's just say that while chasing goats never became a fitness craze, it still warrants a few half points above a 1… you know… for the effort.

SCORE: 2.5

Mettle of Honor:

Harrison did serve as a volunteer in the Civil War and

commanded a brigade that participated in several battles. For that, always , we give points for courage.

SCORE: 6

WhAR: 13

OVERALL RANKING: #34

John Tyler

HEIGHT: 6′
WEIGHT: 160
COLLEGE: William & Mary
SPORTS: None

WHEN IT COMES to a presidential biographer describing the appearance of their subject, I have to acknowledge Robert Seager, the author of "And Tyler Too: A Biography of John and Julia." He wrote one of the most concise, cutting, belittling and highly informative descriptions of a POTUS's physical appearance that I read during my time researching this project.

His portrait of our 10th president John Tyler begins with a light jab:

"Physically, he was never robust."

Okay. So far, so good. That's a fairly polite way of saying that Tyler wasn't a big, strong guy. That's fine. But then Seager kicks it up a notch.

"He was always much too thin…"

Hmmm… "Much too thin" is another way of saying "weak." We've moved out of the polite zone and on to a personal assessment. Then, Seager rips open the curtain on Tyler's medical issues.

"Throughout his life he was highly susceptible to severe gastric upsets…"

Whoa, whoa, whoa… So he was not robust, he was gaunt, and he had an upset stomach all the time. Well, then — not exactly the picture of health. Fine. We got it. Point taken. Nobody was going to mistake John Tyler for Hercules. But just in case you still weren't convinced, Seager goes in for the kill:

"…and to frequent attacks of diarrhea."

Um. Wow. That's just a complete and total takedown of a man

in two sentences. In layman's terms, Seager is saying that Tyler was a skinny wimp who pooped a lot.

Not exactly a winning combination for a human, let alone a president, let alone as an illustration of athletic ability for the purposes of this book.

Unfortunately, after extensive research and study, it appears that outside of frequent bowel movements, Tyler wasn't fond of much physical movement. It's hard to be a good athlete if you're completely lacking any athleticism.

BUT, you know where he wasn't lacking? In the bedroom. Hey-oh! Tyler's most impressive achievement may be that he had more children than any other president — tallying 15 offspring! He had eight children with his first wife and seven with his second.

WhAR (White House Athlete Ranking)

Executive Power
Nope.

SCORE: 1

Running Ability
Another zero here, too.

SCORE: 1

Fit for Office
Another donut here.

SCORE: 1.5

Executive Achievement
Sorry, nope.

SCORE: 2

Mettle of Honor:

Nope.

SCORE: 1

WhAR: 6.5

OVERALL RANKING: #41

CHAPTER 3:
LAME DUCKS

Thomas Jefferson

HEIGHT: 6'2½"
WEIGHT: 180 (estimated)
COLLEGE: William & Mary, founded the University of
   Virginia
SPORTS: Walking, Horse Riding

IMAGINE A POLITICAL career so chock full of accomplishments that you leave the fact that you were president of the United States off of your epitaph in favor of your other greatest hits — being the author of the Declaration of Independence, founding the University of Virginia, and writing the statute of Virginia. That's what Thomas Jefferson did. First and foremost, he was a man of letters, which is why I was not surprised to learn in my research that when it came to exercise, Jefferson, as we'd say today, had some thoughts. In fact, he had a lot of thoughts. Here are a few from various correspondence and writings.

Give about two of them [hours] every day to exercise; for health must not be sacrificed to learning. A strong body makes the mind strong.

As far as what kind of exercise Jefferson recommended, he was an absolute believer in the power of walking:

The object of walking is to relax the mind. You should therefore not permit yourself even to think while you walk. But divert your attention by the objects surrounding you. Walking is the best possible exercise. Habituate yourself to walk very far.

And here's another quote on walking and how it compares to

other "forms" of exercise, namely riding a horse and being in a carriage, which clearly has no physical value:

> *The sovereign invigorator of the body is exercise, and of all the exercises walking is best. A horse gives but a kind of half exercise, and a carriage is no better than a cradle. No one knows, till he tries, how easily a habit of walking is acquired. A person who never walked three miles will in the course of a month become able to walk 15 or 20 without fatigue. I have known some great walkers and had particular accounts of many more; and I never knew or heard of one who was not healthy and long lived.*

Hey, have I mentioned that Jefferson enjoyed walking? I have? I know what you're thinking: "Did old TJ enjoy any other forms of physical activity?" In short, no. He was pro-walking and anti-everything else. And now you're thinking, "This is probably because Jefferson lived in a time before most organized sports. Surely he would have enjoyed football or pick-up hoops or soccer or something like that." Again, the answer would be no. While Americans in Jefferson's era didn't have AAU basketball or the World Cup, they did have sports — it's just that our third president loathed them.

"Games played with the ball and others of that nature, are too violent for the body and stamp no character on the mind," he wrote, as he dismissed nearly every popular modern athlete and sport that would pop up for the next 250 years. Something tells me that Jefferson and Vince Lombardi wouldn't have gotten along very well.

Taking all of this into consideration, I'd say that while Jefferson understood the value of exercise, wrote about it eloquently and clearly practiced it, he was a one-dimensional athlete and his activity of choice was the easiest activity possible: walking.

WhAR (White House Athlete Ranking)

Executive Power

Jefferson was tall and lanky, which gives him a leg up on some of the shorter presidents in the previous section. Judging from descriptions of him, it's fair to say that he possessed slightly more strength than the average president, but not much.

SCORE: 3

Running Ability

As we covered, he was a lifelong walker and horse rider. He has no other physical hobbies to offset these things, so we can only work with what we've got.

SCORE: 4

Fit for Office

Jefferson maintained his walking routine throughout his presidency, which means he made the effort to stay in shape and keep his body strong, living by his own code: "If the body be feeble, the mind will not be strong."

SCORE: 3.5

Executive Achievement

"I'm walking here! I'm walking here!" Is that an achievement?

SCORE: 2.5

Mettle of Honor:

For consistency, I'm giving points here for the fact that if Jefferson and his fellow Founding Fathers had lost the Revolutionary War or been captured during it, they likely would've been hanged for treason. Facing that fact is certainly tough, though not technically an athletic feat.

SCORE: 3

WhAR: 16

OVERALL RANKING: #29

Franklin Pierce

HEIGHT: 5'10"
WEIGHT: 170
COLLEGE: Bowdoin College
SPORTS: Military, Horse Riding

SOMETIMES PRESIDENTIAL NICKNAMES instill reliability (Old Hickory), and sometimes they instill force (Theodore Rex). But in the case of Franklin Hyde Pierce, the nickname "Fainting Frank" instilled neither. Pierce earned this unfortunate moniker when he fell off his horse during the Mexican-American War and passed out from the pain of his broken leg. He recovered enough to ride the next day, only to pass out again. While Pierce gets credit for volunteering to serve in the military, he earned the appointment through his political connections and entered the war as a brigadier general commanding 2,000 men — all while having no military experience.

When researching the early life of our 14th president, I found shockingly little written about his activities outside of school. He was considered to be very smart as well as an outstanding orator. He was described as handsome and charming and, when given the opportunity, he could be quite the party guy.

The first time this little tidbit popped up was when reading about his initial semester at Bowdoin College in Maine, when his taste for a social life took priority over his studies and he plummeted to last in his class. Then again, he began college at 15 years old. Who knows how far most of us would have strayed from our school work if we were on our own at that age. Pierce eventually got his act together and finished fifth in his class.

The second time that Party Guy Pierce reared his ugly head a la Will Ferrell's Frank the Tank was after he was elected to the

House of Representatives in his early 30s, and he had to live in Washington, D.C. According to the Miller Center, at the time D.C. was "an unpleasant place with ill-smelling swamps and political intrigue. Politicians serving there lived mostly in shabby boarding houses. Bored and homesick, many found comfort in alcohol. Drinking quickly became a problem for Pierce. Before long, stories of his partying and drunken escapades were a staple of the capital's grapevine."

What does this have to do with President Pierce's athletic ability? Well… not much, actually. But there is scant evidence that he had any interest in sports or leisurely physical activities. I was hoping to find a story in which Pierce perhaps went streaking through the capital after a bender, but alas, it does not exist.

All of this is to write that just like on the lists of the greatest presidents politically, Pierce will be relegated to the bottom of the POTUS list athletically as well.

WhAR (White House Athlete Ranking)

Executive Power

Franklin Pierce was a notch above average height for his day, and the same with his weight. All we can do is guess that he was neither strong, nor weak, and that he possessed perfectly average and non-distinct strength.

SCORE: 3

Running Ability

The falling-off-a-horse incident doesn't help here — especially during an era when horse riding was considered a top athletic skill.

SCORE: 1

Fit for Office

There's nothing to judge this category on so we'll go with a 1.

SCORE: 1

Executive Achievement

Sorry.

SCORE: 1

Mettle of Honor:

For consistency, I'm giving points here for the fact that Pierce volunteered to serve his country during a war.

SCORE: 3

WhAR: 9

OVERALL RANKING: #36

Andrew Johnson

HEIGHT: 5'10"
WEIGHT: 170 (estimated)
COLLEGE: none
SPORTS: none

SOME MEN ARE meant to wear athletic uniforms, while others are meant to sew them. Having spent his early years as a tailor, Andrew Johnson belonged to the latter group. Johnson usually ranks among the least popular presidents in polls due to his impeachment and his mishandling of the Reconstruction. Unfortunately, without any athletic accomplishments to his name, he's doomed to the basement here as well.

To be fair, Johnson was born into poverty, his father died while trying to rescue two drowning men when he was 3 years old, and at the young age of 14 he apprenticed — or more accurately, was forced to work — for a local tailor. The work consumed his life and left no time for school or any kind of education, including formal lessons on basics like reading and math. After two years with the tailor, Johnson and his brother, who was also an apprentice, ran away never to return, despite a $10 reward offered by the tailor to anyone who found the boys.

After some time on the run, Johnson and his brother opened up their own tailor shop. When he turned 18, he married 16-year-old Eliza McCardle, who was well educated and taught him how to read and write.

Four years later at the ripe age of 22, he'd be mayor of the town of Greenville, North Carolina. This began his political ascension over the decades, which led all the way to the White House, first as Abraham Lincoln's vice president and then as his successor after Lincoln was assassinated. Along the way he was a congressman, a governor, a military governor, and a senator. Yes, the list of John-son's accomplishments is long, but distinguished. (And yes, it was a lot of build-up for that joke, but it was worth it — thanks for hanging in there.)

While none of the above has anything to do with athleticism, there is one thing that does tie Johnson to sports: He was the first president to love baseball, and the first to invite a baseball team to the White House. He was even the special guest of honor in August 1867 at the new ballpark for the National Baseball Club of Washington.

Several articles from his time in office talk about his love of baseball, including one game where he "set the whole White House entourage up on plush straight back chairs along the first base line and that day became the first President to watch an inter-city baseball game."

Sport magazine wrote, "He became so caught up with the prospect of a two inter-city match between the Washington Nationals, Philadelphia Athletics and Brooklyn Atlantics that he gave government clerks and employees time off to watch."

By the end of his presidency he had accepted more than 20 honorary ball club memberships, which is a far cry from playing in the pros, but at least shows a passion for sports.

WhAR (White House Athlete Ranking)

Executive Power

Johnson was an average-sized guy for his time. He was neither a soldier nor an outdoorsman, so there is very little case to be made for his potential strength.

SCORE: 1

Running Ability

Let's assume that a love of baseball gave Johnson a hankering for other games throughout his life, and that he perhaps played in a few along the way. Or at least he played catch.

SCORE: 1

Fit for Office

The cabinet is bare.

SCORE: 1.5

Executive Achievement

Watching baseball isn't the same as *playing* baseball, but I'd like to believe he took a few hacks during batting practice and maybe shagged a few fly balls on the White House lawn.

SCORE: 2

Mettle of Honor:

Tailoring isn't really associated with toughness, and it was hard to find anything else in Johnson's record that indicates his physical fortitude.

SCORE: 1

WhAR: 6.5

OVERALL RANKING: #41

Calvin Coolidge

HEIGHT: 5'10"
WEIGHT: 169
COLLEGE: Amherst College
SPORTS: Fishing

WHEN YOU HEAR someone mention a mechanical bull or horse, what images come to mind, and what kind of people do you picture riding it?

Yes, cowboys, for sure. Also, tourists at state fairs and carnivals; kids at theme parks; and of course, how could we leave out men and women at rodeo-themed bars across the country who have had a few too many shots of tequila and are just waiting to hop on, grab hold and get tossed on their butts in front of all their laughing friends. Ahhh... good times.

You know what image likely doesn't come to mind? And would never in a million years come to your mind prior to reading this?

How about the image of our 30th president Calvin Coolidge riding one several times a day in the White House for exercise?

Oh, you didn't know that "Silent Cal" was so upset over the Secret Service insisting that he no longer ride real horses (due to safety concerns) that a friend bought him an "electric horse" for the Oval Office.

According to Eliza McGraw's article in the *Washington Post,* "The horse looked like a barrel with a neck, and it was made of wood, metal and leather. The rider used a saddle, and electricity powered the horse. You pushed a button to vary gaits, from a trot to a gallop. It was not unlike a Jazz Age exercise bike: something users kept at home and hopped on when they found time to work out."

Coolidge rode his electric horse, nicknamed Thunderbolt

(awesome, right?), three times a day — in the morning, after lunch and after work was over.

And here's a fun fact: That particular electric horse was invented by John Harvey Kellogg of Kellogg's cereal fame.

Aside from fake-horse riding, Coolidge was fond of taking walks in the afternoon before his daily nap, which he refused to give up, even as the leader of the United States. He also took up fly fishing while he was in office and it became one of his passions, once stating about fishing and hunting, "These are true outdoor sports in the highest sense, and must be pursued in a way that develops energy, perseverance, skill, and courage of the individual. They call for personal direction, and cannot be taken up vicariously. There is a great wealth of life and experience in this field, which is never exhausted, and always fresh and new. It is accompanied by traits of character, which make a universal appeal."

Coolidge did not have such glowing remarks about baseball, although he attended 10 games while in office for political reasons, threw out the first pitch six times, and in 1925 handed Walter Johnson his MVP Award. His wife Grace was the real fan in the family, so much so that Bucky Harris, the manager of the Washington Senators during their glory days, once said that Grace was "the most rabid fan I ever knew in the White House."

The other sport that was blowing up during Coolidge's tenure in Washington, D.C. was golf. Once again, it was expected that Coolidge would play rounds with notable individuals for the optics and politics of it, and he miserably obliged. The stories of his futility on the links are scattered all over the papers of his era, with the gist being that it would often take him upward of 10 shots just to reach the green. If there were any doubts about his ill feelings for the game, his final gesture in D.C. should remove them.

When his term was up and it was time for him and Grace to

remove all of their personal belongings from the White House, they cleared out the entire place, save for one item: his golf clubs, which he left for his successor Herbert Hoover.

WhAR (White House Athlete Ranking)

Executive Power

Calvin Coolidge was a slight man who enjoyed sports that didn't require too much strength. Although, if he rode Thunderbolt on *gallop* more than he did on *trot*, we should give out points accordingly.

SCORE: 2

Running Ability

It appears that between long walks and horse riding, Coolidge figured he had his exercise bases covered. Neither of these required elite athletic skill, but they are physical activities.

SCORE: 3

Fit for Office

Considering how little thought many POTUSes gave to their health while in office, we have to give credit to Coolidge for installing Thunderbolt and riding that electric horse several times a day to break a sweat. If it truly was the exercise bike of the 1920s, then good for him and major points are awarded.

SCORE: 5

Executive Achievement

Fly fishing isn't so much an athletic sport as it is a skill, but learning how to do it and do it well should count for something.

The same goes for throwing out a half-dozen first pitches, even though those may have been the only six throws of his life.

SCORE: 2.5

Mettle of Honor:

This is the one area where a lack of military experience and a lack of participation in physical sports prevent me from pushing Coolidge past the dreaded 1.

SCORE: 1

WhAR: 13.5

OVERALL RANKING: #33

Harry Truman

HEIGHT: 5'9"
WEIGHT: 167
COLLEGE: Kansas City Law School (never graduated)
SPORTS: Walking

AT AN EARLY age, Harry Truman was advised by his doctor to avoid sports on account of his poor eyesight, which was 20/50 in his right eye and 20/400 in his left (just above the legal standard for blindness). His main hobbies growing up were music, reading and history, so whereas the legends of great athletes are comprised of stories of young men getting up at the crack of dawn to run sprints or shoot jumpers, Truman famously got up at 5 a.m. every day as a boy to practice the piano.

This isn't to suggest that Truman didn't enjoy physical activity or that he lacked a sense of adventure. When it came time for young Harry to go to college, he applied to the United States Military Academy but was once again stymied because of his poor eyesight. He joined the National Guard instead, and when World War I rolled around and he had to take the eye test again, he passed by memorizing the chart ahead of time.

Truman worked his way up to the rank of captain while he was in the service, then later opened a haberdashery (such a great word) in Kansas City (which went bankrupt due to the Great Depression) before settling on politics (smart move).

Vice President Truman assumed the presidency upon Franklin Roosevelt's death, 82 days into his fourth term. Truman had always been a creature of habit, but now that he was president, his daily routine was to be scrutinized and studied for posterity.

In terms of exercise, walking was Truman's preferred workout.

"I walk early to get a chance to think over things and get ready for the work day," he said.

But unlike other presidents who took leisurely strolls, Truman was a stickler for not only the distance he strolled but the pace as well. Papers posted at the Harry S. Truman Library Museum website, as well as in other articles I found, state his preference for walking at exactly 120 steps per minute for one-and-a-half to two miles every day.

"Walk as if you have somewhere to go" was his motto.

While he didn't have a pre-workout drink laced with caffeine and Creatine like today's early morning exercisers do, Truman's physician prescribed an amazing concoction for him to start the day with: a shot of bourbon followed by a large glass of orange juice. (Nothing like burping up Maker's Mark and OJ while getting your sweat on.)

In terms of diet, I'll let Truman himself explain the presidential eating plan that kept him fit while running World War II. This is a direct entry from his diary:

"I eat no bread, but one piece of toast at breakfast, no butter, no sugar, no sweets. Usually have fruit, one egg, a strip of bacon, and half a glass of skimmed milk for breakfast, liver and bacon or sweet breads or ham or fish and spinach and another non-fattening vegetable for lunch with fruit for dessert."

Liver and bacon… mmm.

Aside from that, Truman's other major "athletic achievement" was the commissioning and the building of the White House bowling alley.

WhAR (White House Athlete Ranking)

Executive Power

Though not prone to feats of strength or physical sports, any man who starts his day with a shot of bourbon and a quick walk must have some inner power ready to be unleashed.

SCORE: 3

Running Ability

Truman maintained his walking regimen for most of his life as a throwback to his days growing up on the farm. Any conscious effort to stay in shape has to count for something, so I'll count it as a 2.

SCORE: 2

Fit for Office

As a walker in office, Truman falls right into the Coolidge and Taft zone here. Although Coolidge and Taft both tried other forms of exercise, it's the commitment to the pace that gives Harry a decent score here. You try walking at 120 steps per minute (I did, it's actually not very hard).

SCORE: 5

Executive Achievement

While it feels odd to give Truman a low score on anything involving achievement since he oversaw the United States' victory in World War II, when it comes to athletic achievement, the best we've got is the installation of a bowling alley, which itself is more of a physical activity than a sport.

SCORE: 2.5

Mettle of Honor:

Truman served in the National Guard and in the Army during World War I, then as president during World War II. What he lacked in physically tough achievements, he made up for in mentally tough ones.

SCORE: 5

WhAR: 17.5

OVERALL RANKING: #26

Lyndon Johnson

HEIGHT: 6'3"
WEIGHT: 200
COLLEGE: Southwest Texas State Teachers College
SPORTS: None

LET'S START WITH the positive: In terms of an off-the-field legacy in sports, Lyndon Johnson has some strong credentials, most notably when it comes to the organization now known as the President's Council on Sports, Fitness and Nutrition. The council was founded by President Eisenhower in 1956 and was originally called the President's Council on Youth Fitness. Then, when John F. Kennedy took office, he removed the "youth fitness" part and made it the President's Council on Physical Fitness in order to include all age groups.

JFK and Ike, as you'll learn later, were both excellent athletes across a multitude of sports, which is why it's somewhat shocking that of the three presidents involved in getting the Council off the ground, LBJ was the one who added sports. He officially changed the name to the President's Council on Physical Fitness and Sports, and also established the President's Physical Fitness Award for exceptional achievement by 10- to 17-year-old boys and girls.* He also named baseball Hall of Famer Stan Musial as the council's chair and consultant to the president.

Why is this shocking?

It's shocking because, athletically speaking, LBJ couldn't hold Kennedy's or Eisenhower's jock. Unlike his two immediate predecessors, Johnson didn't play a sport in college, and even if he had, I'm not sure how the Southwest Texas State Teachers College would have fared against Harvard or West Point back in the day. He did pitch, catch and play first base on his high school baseball team while also playing basketball (he was 6-foot-3), but it seems his athletic career stopped after graduation.

Prior to his political career, Johnson spent time doing manual labor on a road crew and fell into some bad habits, including drinking and fighting, which ultimately led to an arrest. After bottoming out, he took stock of his life and decided to enroll in the Teachers College mentioned above, which led to a job as a teacher and then as an aide to a U.S. Congressman. From that point on, he'd be known as a workaholic who gave himself little time to exercise or even watch sports, aside from attending a few baseball games.

By 1955, nearly a decade before he would become president, he suffered a massive heart attack that nearly killed him. He swore off cigarettes after that and lost some weight, but exercise and regular workouts were never in the cards for much of his political career.

Seemingly, the only exercise he got while in the White House was during his extracurricular activities with the younger ladies on staff. In this area (that would be adultery), LBJ, according to his own accounts, was not only on par with JFK, but he claims to have surpassed him. One legendary story involved Johnson listening to people talk about JFK's female conquests. He eventually was fed up enough to pound his fists on the desk and yell, "Why, I had more women on accident than he ever had on purpose!"

There's no way to know for sure who wins this match-up, but Johnson did have a buzzer installed in the Oval Office so that the Secret Service could warn him if his wife, the famous Lady Bird Johnson, was heading his way.

WhAR (White House Athlete Ranking)

Executive Power

Lyndon Johnson stood 6-foot-3 and weighed between 200 and

210 pounds, depending on the source. He was a confrontational guy who, as we mentioned, worked on a road crew and got into fights as a youth. Although he didn't work out, I'm giving him an above average score here for what appears to be some natural big guy power.

SCORE: 6

Running Ability

During Johnson's run-up to the White House, he was so focused on work that he left little time for anything else, as evidenced by his heart attack, which wasn't a great indicator of physical prowess.

SCORE: 2

Fit for Office

Shagging interns and secretaries doesn't equate to a W.O.D., unfortunately.

SCORE: 2

Executive Achievement

While not a physical achievement, Johnson's work to expand the President's Fitness Council to include sports should count for something.

SCORE: 2.5

Mettle of Honor:

Johnson went on one bombing run in World War II, but it is portrayed in most accounts as a formality to earn his combat stripes. His performance as a fighter and on a road crew is what gives him a few points here above the standard military service bump.

SCORE: 4

WhAR: 16.5

OVERALL RANKING: #28

James Buchanan

HEIGHT: 6'
WEIGHT: 170 (estimated)
COLLEGE: Dickinson College
SPORTS: none

NOBODY REMEMBERS WHO played shooting guard for the Chicago Bulls before Michael Jordan. Nobody remembers who played left field for the Red Sox before Ted Williams. And nobody remembers who was president before Abraham Lincoln. That honor falls to James Buchanan, the ultimate presidential bench warmer.

Old Buck did serve as a private in a light dragoon unit defending Baltimore against the British when they invaded during the War of 1812. Aside from that honor, he is consistently listed as one of the worst presidents of the United States. Ever. Making things even lamer, Buchanan was the only president who served in the military and wasn't an officer.

Even his contemporaries didn't respect him much. In fact, in one of the sharpest insults ever hurled from one man who would become president to another man who would become president, Andrew Jackson coined emasculating nicknames for both Buchanan and his then-roommate, William Rufus King, referring to them as "Miss Nancy" and "Aunt Fancy." Not exactly a ringing endorsement of a man's grit.

The only area of Buchanan's life in which he appeared to excel in comparison to other presidents was his capacity to down alcohol. Though not an alcoholic (at least they wouldn't have called him that in the mid-1800s), Buchanan was fond of Madeira wine, sherry and rye whiskey. As a senator, he had a standing order with his favorite liquor store in Washington, D.C.of 10 gallons of whiskey per week.

John W. Forney, a journalist and politician, once described Buchanan's taste for alcohol by writing, "The Madeira and sherry that he had consumed would fill more than one old cellar, and the rye whiskey that he has 'punished' would make Jacob Baer's heart glad." Jacob Baer was a whiskey maker.

Forney said he was astonished at how lucid Buchanan was following his "punishment" of so much alcohol. "There was no headache, no faltering steps, no flushed cheek," he wrote. "Oh, no! All was as cool, calm and cautious and watchful as the beginning."

WhAR (White House Athlete Ranking)

Executive Power

Buchanan seemed to have handled himself well in hand-to-hand combat as a young man, and he stood 6 feet tall so he wasn't a small guy. Also, he could handle the highest-proof alcohol imaginable, which implies some intestinal strength. All of that is to say we'll give him a courtesy 2.5 in the strength department.

SCORE: 2.5

Running Ability

Aside from his skirmish in Baltimore, I didn't dig up any exercise, workout or fitness habits to speak of.

SCORE: 1

Fit for Office

If hammering whiskey was a sport, Buchanan would get a 10 here for his performance in office. It isn't, so he doesn't.

SCORE: 1

Executive Achievement

Standing by while the country plunged into the Civil War is not an achievement on the political side. Drinking gallons of whiskey every week is not an accomplishment on the health side. So we're left with a 1.

SCORE: 1

Mettle of Honor:

I'll give old Buck a 3 for his work in the light dragoon, but that's it.

SCORE: 3

WhAR: 8.5

OVERALL RANKING: #37

Richard Nixon

HEIGHT: 5'11½"
WEIGHT: 173
COLLEGE: Whittier College, Duke Law
SPORTS: Football, Baseball, Track

ON ONE HAND, I want to give President Nixon credit for playing college football. On the other hand, he played for a small school (Whittier College) whose nickname didn't exactly strike fear into the hearts of opponents (the Poets), and he never made it past the third string as a guard. When Michael Beschloss interviewed one of Nixon's teammates for an article in *The New York Times,* the teammate said that Nixon was cannon fodder who "wasn't cut out to play the sport."

The future president also played baseball and ran track at Whittier, before attending Duke Law School through a scholarship program affectionately known as "the meat grinder" for how difficult it was. It was at Duke where Nixon earned two of his famous nicknames, "Gloomy Gus" and "Iron Butt," on account of how much time he spent studying and worrying about his grades. His diet wasn't very good either, as the Duke Law School website says he subsisted largely on Milky Way bars and soup. This is a diet similar to another college legend, Herschel Walker, who claims to have eaten nothing but Snickers bars in school (Walker had a far different physical outcome, as Nixon was described as "thin and ungainly" at that time).

Despite Nixon's actual athletic ability, he was a giant sports nerd who loved football so much he even floated Vince Lombardi as a possible running mate when he was preparing his campaign for president (alas, Vince was a Democrat). In the win column, one of Nixon's most famous supporters during his presidential run was none other than Jackie Robinson.

Nixon famously "called" a play for the Redskins while he was in office, a rumor that was confirmed as true by Buffalo Bills coaching legend and then-Washington assistant Marv Levy. Nixon could also reel off baseball statistics like he was Rain Man, and was once quoted as saying, "I don't know much about politics, but I know a lot about baseball." According to the official White House logs, he attended 11 games during his roughly four years in office.

He also once said that although he enjoyed being president, if he could go back and do it all over again he would rather have been a sportswriter.

When he wasn't watching sports, talking about sports or ordering wiretaps, Nixon "exercised" by using the White House bowling alley.

WhAR (White House Athlete Ranking)

Executive Power

How much power can we imagine Nixon had as a third-string lineman at a Division III school who was referred to as cannon fodder? Not much.

SCORE: 3

Running Ability

Nixon's interest in watching sports far surpassed his time spent playing them after college.

SCORE: 3

Fit for Office

Bowling isn't necessarily considered exercise, and neither is throwing out a few first pitches over the course of four years.

Other than those activities, Nixon was a workhorse who carved out time to watch sports, but not play them.

SCORE: 3

Executive Achievement

Despite his lack of a starring role — or playing time, for that matter — we have to give Nixon credit here for playing three sports in college.

SCORE: 5

Mettle of Honor:

Being a lineman is tough. So is getting blasted every day as a tackling and blocking dummy. I have to give Nixon a few points for putting himself out there and trying to be the Rudy of Whittier College.

SCORE: 3

WhAR: 17

OVERALL RANKING: #27

Part II: The Contenders

Few presidents shied away from a political battle, and most of the presidents in the top half of these rankings had no problem with a real fight either. In fact, some of them would have been right at home in the UFC. James Garfield was a brawler, Teddy Roosevelt was a boxer, and Abraham Lincoln was a street fighter who in his youth wrestled town bullies for fun. Of course, there's more to athleticism than toughness, which is why this group of elite executives includes a marathoner, several college all-stars, and a bona fide NCAA champion.

CHAPTER 4:
WHITE HOUSE WEEKEND WARRIORS

Donald Trump

HEIGHT: 6'3"
WEIGHT: 242
COLLEGE: Fordham and the University of Pennsylvania
SPORTS: Soccer, Football, Baseball, Golf

DONALD TRUMP WAS a star athlete in high school at the New York Military Academy, earning varsity letters in soccer, football and baseball. He is on the record, of course, as stating that he was "always the best athlete," which is probably in the vicinity of truth if we're talking about his specific graduating class. His two best sports were baseball and football.

As a baseball player Trump's fastball could hit the mid-80s on the radar gun, and in a piece of news that is an actual fact, the Philadelphia Phillies and the Boston Red Sox scouted him as a high school first baseman. His classmate and catcher Ted Levine told *Business Insider*, "he could have probably played pro ball as a pitcher. He made my hand black and blue every day."

On the gridiron, Trump admits to being average, and said in an interview at the Pro Football Hall of Fame that he played on a very low level. His greatest achievement may have been the time he tossed a spiral through a small target about 20 yards out before a USFL game and got a high-five from Jim Kelly.

Outside of those two sports, the overriding athletic passion of Trump's life is golf. In addition to owning some of the nicest courses in the country, he is obsessed with the game and has played in foursomes with just about every celebrity or athlete who plays. The website PresidentialGolfTracker.com has him on pace to play 302 rounds of golf in his first term, far surpassing his predecessor Barack Obama, who played 113 times during his first term.

Although an entire book by legendary sportswriter Rick Reilly describes how much Trump cheats on the course and how he consistently makes up his own rules to win matches and championships, he is officially listed as around a 3-handicap. Those who have played with him claim that he does have legitimate talent and knows the game, but his actual score is often hard to decipher. It doesn't help that The Donald refuses to take short putts, and gives himself a 1 once he gets close enough to the pin that he thinks it's a "gimme."

In early 2019, Trump posted a personal-record low score of 68 in the official USGA Golf Handicap Information Network, which immediately had people claiming that he must have cheated.

One of the biggest strikes against Trump as an athlete — and in trying to assess his proper WhAR score — is that other than his high school days and the time he spends golfing, he does not believe in regular exercise. In fact, he believes that exercise is harmful. In a piece by the *Washington Post* titled "Trump Revealed," the writer's research stated that Trump believes the human body is like a battery with a finite amount of energy that can be depleted.

In a profile in *New York Times Magazine*, he said, "All my friends who work out all the time, they're going for knee replacements, hip replacements — they're a disaster." He also claims that standing in front of an audience and talking exerts enough energy to be called exercise.

And since we've brought up several instances where presidents helped found fitness councils and youth sports leagues and were honorary members of pro teams, when it comes to a sporting legacy, we'd be remiss not to bring up Trump's role in submarining the United States Football League, which was thoroughly documented in Jeff Pearlman's great book, *Football For a Buck.*

WhAR (White House Athlete Ranking)

Executive Power

Donald Trump is one of our biggest presidents size-wise, and his early football career and ability to fire a baseball hint at a good amount of natural strength. However, he hasn't put that strength to use in any way other than on the golf course since he was 18. No weight training. Nothing. He gets the minimum points for big guy strength that we've given other presidents, and a couple more for playing football, but that's it.

SCORE: 5

Running Ability

It's hard to give a man a score for staying in shape when he has declared that exercise is a bad thing. He does golf a lot though, so that at least keeps him out of the basement.

SCORE: 3

Fit for Office

Outside of the 300-plus rounds of golf Donald Trump is projected to play in his first term, he has exercised a grand total of zero times.

SCORE: 3

Executive Achievement

This category is interesting for Trump. Being scouted by Major League Baseball teams is a big deal, and so is being a three-sport varsity high school athlete. Unfortunately, we have almost nothing to go on after high school, and because of the sheer number of people who have claimed his golf scores can't be trusted, we have to take any achievements on the links with a grain of salt.

SCORE: 5

Mettle of Honor

Trump didn't serve in the military and his favorite lifelong sport is golf, which doesn't require much physical mettle. The thing that keeps him out of the bottom third is that he did play football for a short time, so that's something.

SCORE: 3

WhAR Score: 19

OVERALL RANK: #24

William Henry Harrison

HEIGHT: 5'8"
WEIGHT: 165 (estimated)
COLLEGE: Hampden-Sydney College
SPORTS: Horse Riding, Soldiering

IF WE WERE ranking "tough guy" presidents instead of athletic presidents, William Henry Harrison would fare much higher against his POTUS pals. The good news is that unlike many of the other Commanders-In-Chief in this chapter, Harrison's lack of an imposing physical appearance and sports-type achievements don't completely banish him to the bottom of the rankings. Harrison was a lifelong soldier who cut his teeth in famous conflicts like the Battle of Fallen Timbers and the Battle of Tippecanoe (after which he earned the nickname Old Tippecanoe). He rose through the ranks from an Army ensign all the way up to a Major General, distinguishing himself through courage, grit and effectiveness as a leader.

Harrison took calculated risks in his personal life as well. After his future father-in-law denied him his future wife's hand in marriage, Harrison waited until his girlfriend's dad was away on business to marry her (a big time flex). And it gets better. When his new father-in-law returned, demanding an explanation as to "How, sir, do you intend to support my daughter?" Old Tippecanoe, ever the soldier, replied, "Sir, my sword is my means of support."

Boom. Such a great line and story — I'm shocked Tarantino didn't use it in one of the *Kill Bill* films.

Alas, great comebacks don't qualify as an analytic in the WhAR, so WHH's excellent reply doesn't help his rankings much. In fact, when it comes to figuring out how to properly rate Harrison using our criteria, we had to do a little guess work.

If you've read David McCullough's book *Pioneers*, you know that life in the U.S. Northwest Territories at the turn of the 19th century was beyond difficult. There were very few established towns. Roads and/or well-worn paths were mostly non-existent. Travel was almost exclusively on horseback, on foot, or occasionally on the Ohio River. There was a constant threat of attack from Indians. Hunting was plentiful, but food storage and food stores were scarce. In short, it wasn't easy for civilians to manage in the 1800s, let alone soldiers who were subsisting on provisions and substandard gear and clothing.

Keeping all of this in mind, we have to assume that for Harrison to excel in the brutal winters and steamy summers of pre-settled Ohio and Indiana, he was physically tough, had above average endurance and strength, and most importantly, stayed in battle-ready shape. Those are the positives that we can rely on.

When it comes to his presidency, there are two glaring negatives.

One, when Harrison took the oath of office at age 68 he was the oldest president ever to be sworn in (and he remained the oldest until Ronald Reagan).

Two, he died from pneumonia barely one month into his term, so we can't really rank how fit he stayed while in office. Bummer. And yet, like the great Army General himself, we soldier on.

WhAR (White House Athlete Ranking)

Executive Power

We have to assume that WHH had above average strength as a soldier, considering he was fond of using his sword and often found himself in combat. Since he wasn't necessarily a big guy, we'll give him a six here.

SCORE: 6

Running Ability

Since we're left with some guesswork in this area, we have to figure that a soldier who was able to excel in the extreme wilderness for long periods of time was incredibly fit.

SCORE: 6

Fit for Office

Not applicable.

SCORE: 0

Executive Achievement

After careful consideration, we'll include his pivotal roles in two major battles and his service in the War of 1812 as achievements. Though not necessarily athletic achievements, his physicality had to have played a pivotal role. This feels like a perfect four.

SCORE: 3.5

Mettle of Honor:

Let's consider "living by your sword as a soldier in the woods of Ohio in 1800" to be a fairly good measurement of overall toughness.

SCORE: 7

WhAR: 21.5

OVERALL RANKING: #23

Woodrow Wilson

HEIGHT: 5'11"
WEIGHT: 170
COLLEGE: Davidson College/ Princeton
SPORTS: Cycling, Baseball, Golf, Football Coach

WOODROW WILSON PLAYED one season of baseball at Davidson College as a center fielder. He was a decent hitter, but according to an early 1960s *Sports Illustrated* interview with the team's captain Robert Glenn, Wilson "would be a good player if he wasn't so damned lazy!" As the author of the piece John Durant pointed out in the article, it was more likely that Wilson was hampered by physical limitations (weakness, poor eyesight) than he was by a lack of effort. Many historians have noted that Wilson was physically slight and suffered occasional bouts of fatigue throughout his childhood. Rather than Charlie Hustle he may have just been Charlie No-Muscle.

Nevertheless, when Wilson transferred from Davidson to Princeton he once again tried out for the baseball team, only this time he didn't make it. Rather than be away from the game, he chose to become the team's assistant manager, and thrived in that position. He also became the secretary of the Football Association, something akin to a coach today. This early managerial experience no doubt helped him prepare for his future position as head coach of the Wesleyan University football team.

Following football and baseball as a fan would remain a lifelong passion for Wilson, but he soon took an interest in what was then a new activity sweeping the nation: bike riding.

As you can imagine, the scholarly and staid Wilson was not one to be caught up in fads, but after endless pestering by his brother Josie via letters such as the following, he was hooked:

"My bicycle tells me to tell you," Josie wrote him, "that it is waiting anxiously for you to mount it next summer as you said you would."

After putting off riding what some called a "velocipede" for as long as he could, Wilson finally hopped on and took to it like a politician kissing babies. In no time, he was going on longer and longer rides, eventually taking part in three European bike tours, the first of which began in Glasgow and ended some 300 miles later in London (there were obviously dozens of stops). The trip prompted Wilson to join the Cyclists Touring Club and he was an avid cyclist from that point on, becoming the first president to own a bicycle in the White House.

As president, Wilson ditched his wheels for little white balls when he took up golf, playing an astonishing 1,000 rounds during his two terms. But despite playing 18,000 holes as president, Wilson's poor eyesight plagued him and he routinely shot over a hundred, with his best rounds being in the low 90s. He even became so addicted to the game that he had the Secret Service paint golf balls black so he could play in the snow during the Washington, D.C. winters.

In addition to golf, his personal physician Rear Admiral Cary T. Grayson insisted that Wilson ride horseback and keep a strict diet to stay in shape during his eight years in office. And yet, despite all the golf, when Wilson stepped down as Commander-In-Chief he reportedly told a friend that the "dream of his lifetime" would be to cycle through France.

WhAR (White House Athlete Ranking)

Executive Power

Wilson clearly enjoyed fitness and exercise, but due to his naturally slight frame, power sports weren't in the cards.

SCORE: 2

Running Ability

A lifelong love of cycling certainly helps Wilson in this category, with his 300-mile tour of Britain as the crowning achievement.

SCORE: 6

Fit for Office

To the extent that golf is exercise, few presidents "exercised" while in office more than Wilson. And when you take into account that he pretty much sucked at golf, that's a lot of swings for one man over eight years. In fact, just for fun, here's a little math: If he played 1,000 rounds of golf in eight years and averaged a score of around 100 per round, that comes out to 100,000 swings (yeah, I know, that includes putts, but we're just spit balling here). At 100,000 swings over eight years, that's 12,500 swings a year, which puts him at 1,000 golf swings a month, which puts him at 260 golf club swings per week of his presidency. If ever there were proof that in some cases the 10,000-hour rule was total BS, this might be it.

SCORE: 5

Executive Achievement

Getting cut from the Princeton baseball team is almost like the opposite of an achievement. So for this category, we're going to have to lean on the leisurely 300-mile bike tour. Doesn't matter how slow the pace, that's still a lot of biking.

SCORE: 5

Mettle of Honor:

Biking at a medium pace isn't very taxing (although covering

300 miles isn't bad). And Wilson doesn't have any war experience or fighting experience to rely on here. Sorry, Woodrow.

SCORE: 4

WhAR: 22

OVERALL RANKING: #22

William McKinley

HEIGHT: 5'7"
WEIGHT: 185
COLLEGE: Mount Union
SPORTS: Horseback riding, swimming, ice skating,

"COFFEE BILL," A.K.A. William McKinley, was known for his extreme courage as a soldier and was promoted several times for valor displayed on the battlefield during the Civil War — he moved up from private to a Brevet Major by the end of the conflict. But about that "Coffee Bill" nickname. McKinley earned it during the bloodiest and most horrific clash in the Civil War, the Battle of Antietam. An article on the Canton Republic website (the news source of McKinley's hometown) explained the account below. It's important to keep in mind that McKinley's regiment had been marching all night toward the enemy position, and when the skirmish started they were ordered to attack. None of the troops had eaten since the day before (and you'll see why this is relevant).

> *"Left at the rear about 2 miles behind the fighting was a 19-year-old schoolteacher from Niles, Ohio. It was William McKinley who had enlisted as a private. The young man now had the job of Commissary Sergeant. He was responsible for feeding the men. As he sat in the warm sun and listened to the horrific battle noise from the battlefield, he saw men coming back. They were scared and confused. He had a great idea. He started brewing coffee and putting food into two wagons. He rounded up a couple of old mules and started out toward the battlefield with his supplies."*

Christopher Kenney, director of education for the William

McKinley Presidential Library & Museum, pointed out that "McKinley's actions came during the 'chaos of the battle,' and he may have 'gone against orders' in setting up what amounted to a front lines food camp."*

"He took the supplies through the fighting," Kenney said. "The men doing battle took turns falling back to get food. That gave them the nourishment they needed to continue in battle."

Prior to playing a crucial role in the most critical battle of the Civil War, McKinley spent time fishing, hunting, ice skating, horseback riding and swimming. Standing at only 5-foot7, he was one of our shorter presidents but was clearly fleet of foot as a young man. As he got older, his activity levels decreased and his waistline increased, so much so that Potus.com has him listed as the eighth heaviest President at 199 pounds.

This isn't to say that McKinley didn't leave a lasting legacy when it comes to athletics. In 1868, the future Commander-in-Chief cut his teeth as president of the YMCA, which, as we all know, is home to untold numbers of gyms, pick-up hoops leagues, pools and other sports. Like several of the other kind-of/sort-of athletic presidents we've mentioned, McKinley did make it a habit to take long walks around D.C. while he was in office. But that counts as exercise, not as athleticism.

Kenney was interviewed by Gary Brown of the Canton Republic for this piece.

WhAR (White House Athlete Ranking)

Executive Power

If you're standing at 5-foot-7 and 200 pounds, you are either a power lifter, a bodybuilder, or more likely a guy with a belly who needs to lose 25 pounds. Or you're William McKinley. By all accounts, he was considered a stout guy rather than a chubby guy, and considering his willingness to perform in battle, we'll give him medium-guy strength.

SCORE: 5

Running Ability

McKinley was a very active kid and young adult, and he participated in a host of outdoor activities. We don't know how fast of a swimmer he was or what his horse riding skills were, but having these things on his résumé, along with his top-notch soldiering during the Civil War, moves him out of the basement in this category.

SCORE: 4

Fit for Office

We've been here before. We'll count McKinley as one of our "walking while in the White House" guys and move on with it.

SCORE: 3

Executive Achievement

In terms of specific athletic achievements, the feats that earned him the nickname "Coffee Bill" are the closest things we could find that fall in this category. Wrangling food. Loading wagons. Organizing mules. Dodging bullets and cannons. And doing all of it during the Battle of Antietam is definitely an achievement that deserves recognition both athletically and militarily.

SCORE: 4.5

Mettle of Honor:

McKinley was considered a tough guy as a soldier and as a president. Unfortunately, he was shot by an anarchist at the

Pan-American Exposition in Buffalo, New York early in his second term. After a surgeon removed one bullet, McKinley hung on for eight days before succumbing to gangrene from the second bullet still lodged in his body. Physicians attributed his robust health as the reason he was able to survive for so long after the assassination attempt. That has to count for something when it comes to grit.

SCORE: 6

WhAR: 22.5

OVERALL RANKING: #21

CHAPTER 5:
NATIONAL TREASURES

Andrew Jackson

HEIGHT: 6'1"
WEIGHT: 160
COLLEGE: none
SPORTS: Dueling, Brawling, Scrapping, Fighting

BEING A FIT sportsman in the "Age of Jackson" meant excelling at three things: horse-riding, dueling and fighting. As evidenced by the fact that our seventh president has an entire age named after him, Old Hickory must have been the ultimate triple threat. Historians conservatively estimate that he won at least 14 duels, but the number may actually be well above 50. Whatever the real stat is, Jackson always managed to survive, though he lived much of his life with two bullets lodged in his body.

One of those bullets entered his chest during a duel with Charles Dickinson, a well-known marksman who shot Jackson, but not before the future president could fire off a few rounds and kill him. It took Jackson several months to recover from the wound, but it did not deter him from accepting future challenges.

When a gun wasn't available, Jackson beat up people with his bare hands or, most famously, with his cane. This incident occurred when a man named Richard Lawrence jumped out of a crowd with two pistols aimed at Jackson (the first presidential assassination attempt; there's a trivia question for you). When the guns didn't immediately fire, Jackson bull-rushed him and beat him to the ground — stopping only when none other than Davy Crockett pulled Lawrence away. Like a 19th century Chuck Norris, Andrew Jackson was never scared half to death — death was scared half to Andrew Jackson.

Jackson did not have an easy life early on. The British took him as a prisoner during the Revolutionary War when he was only a teenager and he contracted small pox while in captivity with his brother (who died). When he was finally set free his mother died and he became an orphan. After that he took to gambling, drinking, dueling and chasing ladies (can you blame him?).

It wasn't until the War of 1812 that he found his calling as a leader and a General, winning a host of important battles, and his life took a turn toward a road to the White House.

Jackson was known for his white-hot temper and his courage, which certainly have a place in duels and war, but we have little else to go on in terms of his athleticism.

WhAR (White House Athlete Ranking)

Executive Power

Jackson was tall and thin, and rather than engaging in hand-to-hand combat he preferred to fight with guns. It's hard to determine his overall strength, although we can be sure that he wasn't a weakling. We'll have to assume that in order to overcome several bullets hitting his body during duels he had enough lean muscle to protect his vital organs, therefore he was at least of average strength.

SCORE: 5

Running Ability

Is dueling exercise? Probably not (although it certainly would raise your heart rate). Jackson's only other activity that would qualify here is horse riding, for which he was likely in the middle of the pack, presidentially speaking.

SCORE: 5

Fit for Office

Jackson was known more for his gambling and "man of the

people" lifestyle while in office, rather than any kind of health or wellness regimen.

SCORE: 3

Executive Achievement

Allegedly winning 50 duels is quite an accomplishment, but it's not exactly a measure of speed, size or strength.

SCORE: 3

Mettle of Honor:

Jackson's willingness to put his life on the line for his country (War of 1812) and for his pride (dozens of duels) certainly indicates that he was tougher than most. And the fact that he walked around for most of his life with multiple bullets in his body has major street cred when we're talking about mettle.

SCORE: 7

WhAR: 23

OVERALL RANKING: #20

John Quincy Adams

HEIGHT: 5'7"
WEIGHT: 175
COLLEGE: Harvard
SPORTS: Walking, Swimming

IF JOHN ADAMS was our first Walker-In-Chief, his son John Quincy, our sixth president, would add another leg of the triathlon and became the first Swimmer-In-Chief. Like his father, he was fond of a good stroll, especially in the winter, but come spring and into late fall, JQA was the Michael Phelps of the capitol, taking to the Potomac River for morning swims every single day before dawn. Fortunately, John Quincy kept a meticulous daily journal from his teenage years all the way into his 80s, so we have at our disposal his first-hand thoughts and accounts of his exercise routine.

"I rise usually between four and five," John Quincy wrote in his journal. *"I walk two miles, bathe in Potowmack* (sic) *river, and walk home, which occupies two hours — read or write, or more frequently idly waste the time till eight or nine when we breakfast..."*

As a young man, John Quincy's swims typically lasted in the range of 20 minutes, but as he got older he gradually increased them to an hour. In fact, he hit the hour mark as a 53-year-old and his doctor advised him to dial it back (advice he didn't follow).

"Dr. Huntt and all my friends think I am now indulging it [swimming] *to excess,"* he writes. *"I never before this day swam an hour at once; and I must now limit my fancies for this habit, which is not without danger — the art of swimming ought in my opinion to be taught as a regular branch of education."*

In another entry, John Quincy explains exactly why he loves the water so much:

"I follow this practice for exercise, for health, for cleanliness and

for pleasure — I have found it invariably conducive to health, and never experienced from it the slightest inconvenience."

In fact, on one occasion when a flimsy boat he was riding on began to fill with water and sink, his swimming habit saved his life, as he was able to swim to shore. The only problem Adams had was that he had become so accustomed to swimming in the nude (yes, all his swimming could be classified as "skinny dipping," a common practice at the time) that he struggled for a bit with the weight of his soaked clothes.

There aren't many people in their 50s and 60s who wake up before dawn to walk and swim for an hour in modern times, let alone in the early 1800s, so we have to give John Quincy his due credit for being a founding member of the 5 a.m. workout club. But like modern celebrities who worship at the altar of sweating before six like The Rock, Jocko Willink, the late, great Jack LaLanne and yours truly, JQA's healthy habit would be completely at home in the early 21st century. One can only imagine that if he were president now, he'd have a massive following on his Instagram page for selfies of him jumping in the river at sunrise, replete with the posting of his morning workouts and motivational quotes and shout outs.

John Quincy Adams also installed the first pool table at the White House, although he got into a bit of trouble with the purchase. According to OurWhiteHouse.org, "Adams initially billed the government for the $61 it cost for the table, cues, and billiard balls, but the public was outraged that he sought tax dollars for such a personal purchase. Adams eventually caved to public dissent and reimbursed the government."

WhAR (White House Athlete Ranking)

Executive Power

When was the last time you tried to swim for an hour straight?

Have you ever? While it would be easy to dismiss John Quincy in the strength category because of his lack of size and fairly portly dimensions, it takes a fair amount of power to fight the current of a river for an hour, so we have to give our respect.

SCORE: 4

Running Ability

This category ranks a president's physical fitness and cardio, both of which John Quincy took an active interest in improving and maintaining throughout his presidency and his life. Of course, he didn't have the benefit of Fitbits and CrossFit and the modern literature on the positive effects of fitness, but he instinctively knew daily exercise was a good thing and he made it a habit to get his "sweat" time in.

SCORE: 5

Fit for Office

If John Quincy had another physical activity to go along with walking and swimming, he may have been in the running for an 8 or 9 here. As it stands, he's sitting pretty with a 7.5, given his devotion to his routine throughout his term.

SCORE: 7.5

Executive Achievement

Not much here in terms of what some of our modern presidents have achieved (marathons, college scholarships, high school championships, etc.), but open-water swimming counts for something.

SCORE: 3

Mettle of Honor:

I can't give him too many endurance points here for his two-mile walks, but as a swimmer myself, I'm partial to anyone who can swim for an hour straight, especially in their 50s.

SCORE: 4

WhAR: 23.5

OVERALL RANKING: #19

Zachary Taylor

HEIGHT: 5'8"
WEIGHT: 150
COLLEGE: none
SPORTS: Military

WHEN ZACHARY TAYLOR was elected president, he was one of the most popular people in the United States — and not just from a voting perspective. The man was a bona fide war hero who saw action in the War of 1812, the Black Hawk War, the Second Seminole War, and the Mexican-American War. Though Taylor was only 5-foot-8 and weighed a buck-fifty, he fought like a man twice his size and had a reputation for joining the front lines with his soldiers, favoring hand-to-hand combat over hanging back on his horse.

Since most of Taylor's battles took place along the borders of America, he faced it all — a barrage of bows and arrows and tomahawks on the frontier, and the standard bullets and gunfire and cannons along the Mexican border. It seemed no matter the battleground, Taylor was fixin' for a fight, which led to one of the great presidential nicknames of all time: Old Rough and Ready.

OR & R (as we call him) spent two-thirds of his life in the military, and we have to extrapolate levels of toughness and athleticism based on his chosen profession and the time period in which he lived. Had he been born in the 21st century, he likely would have gone the route of President Dwight Eisenhower, who played bigger than he was and excelled at team sports as a hard-nosed, scrappy athlete, then transferred that mentality to success in the military. Based on the reports of his fighting style, he might have been an all-state wrestler or mixed martial artist; maybe he would've been a tough-as-nails receiver like Julian Edelman. We can't say for sure, but one thing we do know is that he must have had speed, agility, strength and tenacity to survive 40 years in the army, where he rose to the rank of Major General while making it a point to spend time on the front lines.

In terms of his physical habits or exercise routines once he was in office, unfortunately we don't have much of a sample to look at. After a particularly scorching Fourth of July ceremony in Washington, D.C. during his second year in office, Taylor came down with a stomach bug after eating "large quantities of fruit and drinking ice water." He was dead five days later, having served only 16 months as president.

WhAR (White House Athlete Ranking)

Executive Power

While not a physical specimen by any stretch, winning countless battles in hand-to-hand combat over a 40-year military career certainly proves that Taylor likely fought well above his weight class and was stronger than your average man in the mid-1800s.

SCORE: 5

Running Ability

Much like the rationale in the Executive Power category, the fact that Taylor fought in continuous battles rather than a regulated combat sport with rounds, breaks and referees should obviously not be held against him. In fact, he should get bonus points for having enough cardio and physical fitness to survive four decades of battles.

SCORE: 4.5

Fit for Office

This is a tough one. He passed away so early into his term and he was in his mid-60s when he was elected to office. We'll give him a two, out of respect for his military career.

SCORE: 2

Executive Achievement

Zachary Taylor joined the army to win battles — and that's what he did. Toward the end of his military career, he was often mentioned in the same breath as George Washington and Andrew Jackson, which ranks pretty high as far as an achievement goes (although we have to acknowledge that it doesn't qualify as a true athletic accomplishment).

SCORE: 5.5

Mettle of Honor:

Taylor was flat out tough. I don't think there's any doubt about that. No need to belabor the point and discuss his combat experience here any more.

SCORE: 7

WhAR: 24

OVERALL RANKING: #18

Franklin Roosevelt

HEIGHT: 6'2"
WEIGHT: 188
COLLEGE: Harvard, Columbia Law
SPORTS: Hiking, Swimming

FRANKLIN DELANO ROOSEVELT was the second-most athletic Roosevelt to be president.

If this sounds like a backhanded compliment, it is. And no, I'm not at all taking shots at our longest-tenured Commander-In-Chief for having polio. For those who don't know (and the press in the 1930s and '40s did a magnificent job of covering it up), FDR was stricken with polio when he was 39 years old, rendering him mostly paralyzed from the waist down. He worked tirelessly the rest of his life to walk with crutches, braces and the help of aids, which fooled many people and the general public, but the fact is he relied on wheelchairs and walking props for the latter part of his life.

Clearly, I'm not going to judge FDR's athletic ability based on his adult disability, which he fought against with various exercises and treatments during his whole time in office. Instead, I'm examining FDR's athletic career and overall fitness up to the point of his polio, which gives us roughly four decades to go on.

The good news is that Roosevelt liked sports and attempted to play most of them as a kid. The bad news is that he wasn't very good. At Groton School, which was a small boarding school in Massachusetts for rich kids, young Franklin played football and served as manager of the baseball team. After Groton, he went to Harvard University and was mediocre at every sport. This is how the FDR Foundation describes his college athletic career in an essay on their website:

"He was so-so at golf, so-so at tennis and too light for football,

Teddy Roosevelt's [his cousin] favorite contact sport and the one that mattered most in the turn-of-the-century culture of masculinity. With 150 others Frank tried out for freshman football, but was cut and assigned to the Missing Links, the lightest of eight intramural 'scrub' teams. His teammates elected him captain. 'It is the only [team] composed wholly of freshmen,' he wrote to his parents, 'and I am the only Freshman Captain.'"

Roosevelt did not play ball after his freshman year. Instead, he poured his time and energy into a variety of clubs, classes and projects, including time as an editor and writer for the Harvard Crimson, for which he once wrote that certain linemen on the school's football team were "of a spirit that will not awake till the team is in a desperate crisis, and goes to sleep again when the crisis is fancied to be past."

When he wasn't lamenting his status as a football scrub or bashing the Crimson linemen in print, Roosevelt enjoyed sailing, fishing, hunting, horse riding, and playing golf and tennis. Overall, I give Roosevelt a lot of credit for having an interest in sports and for staying active throughout his life. Even after he was debilitated Roosevelt tried to stay active, mainly through swimming exercises and rehab, which he first did in a therapy pool at his Hyde Park home in New York City and then at an indoor pool built in the White House.

The pool was built following a campaign by the *New York Daily News* to raise funds for the presidential pool, as the public knew that FDR utilized water therapy to alleviate his polio symptoms. The pool opened on June 2, 1933, and according to the White House website was a "rectangular pool, encircled by arched ceilings and high rows of half-mooned windows." The pool was built in the west terrace between the White House and the West Wing.

Party pooper President Richard Nixon built a press room above the old pool while he was in office.

WhAR (White House Athlete Ranking)

Executive Power

FDR was tall and skinny and built like a pole vaulter, foreshadowing his ability as a politician to be a poll vaulter. Due to his overall height and his effort to play football, however, we can't assume he was weak or softer than average. This feels like a perfect place for a 5.

SCORE: 5

Running Ability

During FDR's pre-polio days he was extremely active, enjoying most of the sports that modern presidents enjoyed. While he didn't compete and was more of a casual participant, he gets a solid score here as well.

SCORE: 5

Fit for Office

This category is about how fit a president stayed while in office. Because everything is relative, his commitment to swimming and staying active even though he had polio should be commended and acknowledged here.

SCORE: 5

Executive Achievement

TLC would not have wanted any part of FDR (because they don't want no scrubs, and he was on the scrub football team at

Harvard, so….). But he did play freshman ball and was average at other sports, so I'll give him a slightly below average mark here.

SCORE: 3.5

Mettle of Honor:

Politically, Roosevelt guided the nation through the Great Depression and much of World War II, all while battling the physical limitations and frustrations that went along with his polio affliction. That's pretty damn tough in my book.

SCORE: 6

WhAR: 24.5

OVERALL RANKING: #17

Rutherford B. Hayes

HEIGHT: 5'8½"
WEIGHT: 170
COLLEGE: Kenyon College
SPORTS: Soldiering

DUE TO A slightly overprotective mother, future president and war hero Rutherford B. Hayes was not allowed to play rough sports or be outside alone until he was 10 years old. "Rud," as his mom called him, turned those restrictions into a positive and used the down time to work out his brain, eventually becoming valedictorian of his high school class and earning a spot in Harvard Law School. Hayes was well on his way to becoming a career lawyer when the Civil War started and he decided to volunteer for the Union Army.

"I would prefer to go into it if I knew I was going to die, than to live through and after it without taking any part in it," he said of joining the cause.

Keep in mind that Hayes was in his late 30s and had been out of college for 15 years. He was a husband and a father with three kids and another on the way — which actually might explain why war seemed like a good option (I'm kidding!). Also, he was aware that he had no military experience, so he had to drill with a company known as the Burnet Rifles, which was made up of men who were half his age.

Amazingly, future president William McKinley was in the same regiment — the 23rd Ohio — as Hayes when they were called to war. McKinley was stunned with the transformation that overcame Hayes when it was time for combat.

"His whole nature seemed to change in battle. From the sunny, agreeable, the kind, the generous, the gentle gentleman…he was, once the battle was on, intense and ferocious," McKinley wrote.

He was also a magnet for Confederate bullets — but even they couldn't stop him.

According to the Rutherford B. Hayes Presidential Library and Museum in reference to the Battle of South Mountain in the Antietam Campaign, "Hayes was at the head of the 23rd, spearheading the attack on the Rebel position in Fox's Gap. Two charges pushed the Confederates back, but just as Hayes ordered a third charge, a musket ball fractured his left arm above the elbow, leaving a gaping hole." Hayes survived, thanks to the skill of his brother-in-law Dr. Joseph Webb, his regimental surgeon. He also had a horse shot out from under him, and he took a bullet in the shoulder later in the war, but still he would not leave his troops.

By the end of the Civil War, Hayes had been promoted up the ranks and the Republicans nominated him for the House of Representatives. He refused the nomination, saying, "an officer fit for duty who at this crisis would abandon his post to electioneer for a seat in Congress ought to be scalped."

That sentiment has nothing to do with Hayes' athletic ability or ability as a soldier, but it's a great tough guy quote and I had to include it.

There is very little written about Hayes and his personal life in regards to exercise, so we're going to have to lean heavily on his military exploits to extract what his athletic ability might have been.

WhAR (White House Athlete Ranking)

Executive Power

I don't know the exact amount of strength it takes to be shot in the elbow and shoulder and still continue to perform in battle, so I'll just say that Hayes was likely stronger than average.

SCORE: 6

Running Ability

Despite a lack of evidence of fitness and physical activity for the early part of Hayes' life, the idea of joining an army regiment at 39 or 40, when most modern soldiers are retiring, is impressive. That means when it came to drilling, he was as fit as men half his age. And since he continued to excel as he got older (he was almost in his mid-40s when the Civil War ended), he was like an 1860s version of Brett Favre.

SCORE: 5

Fit for Office

Not much in the way of athletic achievements or exercise while Hayes was in office, unfortunately. We have to ding him here a bit.

SCORE: 3

Executive Achievement

Hayes' achievements are all of the military variety, and that's fine by me. Whereas modern men around the age of 40 are fighting against dad bods, he put his life on the line to end slavery.

SCORE: 5

Mettle of Honor:

As I'm writing this, I'm roughly the age of Hayes when he enlisted, and on most days either my shoulder or knee or back ache for no reason. Why am I bringing this up? Mainly because Hayes was likely dealing with the same everyday over-40 nonsense while also taking bullets in his arm and shoulder — and thriving with the best primitive medicine and pain killers the 1860s had to offer. What I'm saying is, I think Hayes was one tough dude.

SCORE: 6

WhAR: 25

OVERALL RANKING: #16

Ulysses S. Grant

HEIGHT: 5'8½"
WEIGHT: 165
COLLEGE: West Point
SPORTS: Horse Riding

ATHLETICALLY SPEAKING, ULYSSES S. Grant was a one-dimensional phenomenon. He was an average-sized man who barely got in to West Point, and he made little to no physical impression on his peers or his teachers. He was often reprimanded for his sloppy dress and lack of discipline. He didn't excel in fitness drills or training or in any area where individual speed or power may have been helpful. He was unexceptional as a young man walking the campus, and perhaps would have been forgettable if not for one very important fact: Grant was the greatest horse rider West Point and perhaps the entire United States had seen in the 19th century.

When he was 10 years old, he had already built a reputation as the one person in his town who could break and control the mightiest, most unruly horses. At West Point, he was widely regarded as an expert horseman, head and shoulders above his classmates and professors. He even set an equestrian high-jump record as a cadet that lasted for 25 years.

William Conant Church, who was from Grant's hometown, had this to say about him: "The town was full of lively fellows and there were many horses whose owners considered them to be fast; and Grant had that pony… He was in the forefront of any racing that was going on," Church said. "On Saturdays the whole town seemed to get out on Fort Avenue and every man who had a horse took part. Grant had that little black mare and it was a horse of tremendous speed. He was the best horseman I ever saw. He could fly on a horse, faster than a slicked bullet."

During the Civil War, General Horace Porter said, "General Grant was a great rider, simply splendid. He could ride 40 or 50 miles and come in perfectly fresh and tire out younger men."

Corporal M. Harrison Strong echoed that sentiment. "He was a great horseman and sat his horse as if he were part of the horse, all one figure," Strong said. "There was never a movement of any description that was not masterful and graceful. No one ever saw him disturbed in any way, that is, jolted or taken unaware on horseback, whether he was going fast or slow. He was a born horseman."

I could go on. In every account of Grant either at West Point or in battle, someone somewhere throws in a remark about his stellar horsemanship. In regards to giving Grant an overall score as an athlete, in some ways he's like a boxer with one devastating knockout punch. Yes, you can ding him for his lack of footwork or poor defense or not throwing clean combinations, but at the end of the day, he's so good at one thing that it almost makes up for the lack of skills in other areas. And so it goes with Grant as an athlete.

Back in the mid 1900s, a man's skills as a horseman were treated very much like a man's athletic ability would be today. And on the biggest stages (West Point, the Civil War), Grant bested everyone.

WhAR (White House Athlete Ranking)

Executive Power

Grant had enough power at 165 pounds to be known for his expert control of horses that weighed nearly 10 times as much as he did.

SCORE: 5

Running Ability

Grant was an animal lover his whole life, and although horse riding came natural to him, he never stopped honing his craft.

SCORE: 3

Fit for Office

While in office, Grant rode as often as he could to relieve stress — but this unfortunately didn't counteract the other habit he picked up to relieve stress: cigar smoking.

SCORE: 3

Executive Achievement

Setting a high-jump record on a horse at West Point is certainly memorable — somewhat less so than winning the Civil War, however.

SCORE: 5

Mettle of Honor:

There are roughly a thousand descriptions of Grant's courage as a man and as a soldier, all of them describing the fact that he was never rattled, never panicked, and always led with a stone look on his face. But this description is my favorite, from Shelby Foote:

> *Grant the general had many qualities but he had a thing that's very necessary for a great general. He had what they call 'four o'clock in the morning courage.' You could wake him up at four o'clock in the morning and tell him they had just turned his right flank and he would be as cool as a cucumber.*

Four o'clock courage. Awesome.

SCORE: 10

WhAR: 26

OVERALL RANKING: #15

James Monroe

HEIGHT: 6'
WEIGHT: 180 (estimated)
COLLEGE: William & Mary
SPORTS: Soldiering

TODAY'S NFL COMBINE measures an athlete's quickness and agility in a number of ways, from cone drills, to the 40-yard dash, to running a tackling dummy gauntlet in a nice, air conditioned dome. In James Monroe's day, foot speed was measured under fire on the battlefield. If you were too slow to dodge bullets, cannon balls and muskets, you didn't just go undrafted, you went to the afterlife.

During the Battle of Trenton in the Revolutionary War, Monroe was severely wounded in the shoulder, but he refused to come off the battlefield, ultimately leading the charge against British cannon fire and taking their position. Standing at 6 feet tall and, as one observer described, "broad shouldered with a massive, raw boned frame," Monroe had an impressive field presence.

Known as the last "Founding Father" (even though he was 18 when the Declaration of Independence was signed), Monroe was friendly with all the big names of his era. He was commanded by Washington, friends with Lafayette, and mentored by Jefferson. He used his soldiering as a means to rise in the political ranks, which culminated in two terms as President of the United States.

There is very little information about Monroe's physical pursuits beyond his days as a soldier, but his feisty reputation lasted well into his old age. According to the blog "Plodding Through the Presidents," this story perfectly illustrates that point:

"When President Monroe was 73, his Treasury Secretary William Crawford called him a 'damned infernal old scoundrel' and raised his cane as if to strike. Monroe quickly grabbed the tongs from the fireplace to defend himself. Crawford backed down and apologized before the President had a chance to barbecue him."

Fireplace tongs not withstanding, most descriptions of Monroe, especially in his youth, comment on his size and naturally broad shoulders and chest. We'll have to do some creative extrapolating to come up with his official WhAR score.

WhAR (White House Athlete Ranking)

Executive Power

Monroe was a bigger-than-average guy throughout his life, and as we noted, he cut an imposing figure. From that description and considering some of his feats in battle, we can give him a nice score here.

SCORE: 7

Running Ability

Running through bullets in battle is a little different than the running our modern presidents did to score high in this category. We'll give Monroe a few extra points for degree of difficulty.

SCORE: 5

Fit for Office

We don't have a lot to go on here. Monroe didn't leave much of a record of daily walks or horse rides while in office.

SCORE: 3

Executive Achievement

This is another area where, athletically speaking, there isn't much. Even his contemporaries like Washington and Jefferson and Adams left a decent trail of their physical fitness and/or skills in sports. Monroe seemingly didn't have those.

SCORE: 3

Mettle of Honor:

Taking a bullet to the shoulder and continuing to lead his troops in battle — often by running through cannon fire — is good enough for Monroe to prove his grit. Also, threatening to beat up someone with fireplace tongs as a 73-year-old man is pretty strong, too.

SCORE: 10

WhAR: 28

OVERALL RANKING: #14

Herbert Hoover

HEIGHT: 5'11"
WEIGHT: 185
COLLEGE: Stanford University
SPORTS: Hoover-ball

ABNER DOUBLEDAY INVENTED America's pastime but never spent time as commander-in-chief. Dr. James Naismith created basketball but never occupied the Oval Office. Walter Camp is known as the father of American football, but he never sat in the same seat as the father of our country. When it comes to the spawning of a new sport and leading a nation, our 31st president set the precedent. Who was the esteemed No. 31? None other than Herbert Clark Hoover. The sport? Hoover-ball, of course.

If you happened to miss last year's Hooverfest in Iowa (no, seriously) and don't have a clue what Hoover-ball is, here's a quick intro straight from Hoover's Presidential Library and Museum: "[Hoover-ball] is a combination of tennis and volleyball played with a medicine ball … the court is 66 feet by 30 feet, the net is 8 feet high and the medicine ball weighs 6 pounds … teams consist of 2–4 players … and the scoring is exactly like tennis." Why a 6-pound medicine ball? Because throwing a ball heavier than 6 pounds at a president isn't a game, it's an assassination attempt. Also, the 9-pound ball with which they experimented was too heavy to be thrown over the net and caught — the object of the game.

Basically, the game is scored like tennis, except the server throws the ball over the net instead of hitting it with a racket. An opposing team member then has to catch the ball on the fly and return it in one motion. The goal is to toss the ball so no one on the other team can catch it. If the ball hits the ground, the serving side gets the point. You can also get a point if the other team serves it out of bounds or throws the ball into the net. Hoover, who was so punctual that clocks asked *him* what time it was, played every day at 7 a.m. sharp for a half-hour with a group of men dubbed the "Medicine Ball Cabinet." Rumor has it that he canceled only one day of Hoover-ball throughout his presidency — and he did that only because he had to wake up early to write a message to deliver to the Senate.

While the game might sound a little ridiculous, the men who played with Hoover swore it was exhausting. One of his friends, Will Irwin, wrote about it in a 1931 article for *Physical Culture* magazine called "The President Watches His Waistline." He wrote, "It is more strenuous than either boxing, wrestling or football. It has the virtue of getting at nearly every muscle in the body." William Atherton DuPuy, a *New York Times Magazine* reporter (and the man who named the game "Hoover-ball"), wrote the following after taking in a few contests for another 1931 article called "At the White House at 7 a.m.": "Stopping a six-pound ball with steam in back of it, returning it with similar steam, is not pink-tea stuff."

I have no idea what "pink-tea stuff" is, but I'm assuming it's on par with something like basket-weaving or origami.

This means that Hoover-ball was one strenuous, bad-ass sport. In fact, the man who co-invented it, Adm. Joel T. Boone (Hoover's White House physician), figured out exactly how strenuous it was, estimating that playing a half-hour game was three times more exercise than tennis, which makes it 500 times more exercise than Hoover's favorite sport of fishing.

The president was also a huge sports fan, particularly of baseball, and he checked the box scores in the newspaper every morning.

"I grew up on sandlot baseball, swimming holes, and fishing with worms," Hoover remembered.

He also played shortstop for Stanford University's baseball team until he dislocated his finger, which ended his playing days and led to him transitioning to the role of team manager.

According to WhiteHouseHistory.org, as president, Hoover encouraged children to build their character and learn about teamwork through sports.

WhAR (White House Athlete Ranking)

Executive Power

Herbert Hoover is right in the middle of the pack in terms of size and strength, but he gets bonus points for willingly heaving a 6-pound medicine ball over a volleyball net on a regular basis.

SCORE: 6

Running Ability

Prior to taking office, Hoover was a generally active guy who appreciated sports and played them throughout his childhood. Nothing stands out past his short-lived college baseball career in terms of daily routine or accomplishments — that is, until the advent of Hoover-ball. However, his interests and accomplishments lead us to believe that he was likely a better-than-average athlete.

SCORE: 6

Fit for Office

When it comes to staying in shape in the Oval Office, inventing a sport and convincing others to play it with you on a regular basis qualifies for a perfect 10 in our book.

SCORE: 10

Executive Achievement

Not to belabor the point, but did we mention that Hoover had a game named after him that decades later has become popular with CrossFit athletes? We have? Good, because that is one hell of an achievement.

SCORE: 9

Mettle of Honor:

This is definitely an area of weakness for Hoover, who didn't play any of the contact sports and doesn't have any active military or battle experience.

SCORE: 2.5

WhAR: 33.5

OVERALL RANKING: #13

Jimmy Carter

HEIGHT: 5'9"
WEIGHT: 160
COLLEGE: Georgia Institute of Technology, U.S. Naval
Academy
SPORTS: Tennis, Jogging, Swimming, Fishing

JIMMY CARTER IS the Bill Buckner of presidents — but not for the reason you might think. If you know anything about Buckner, the first thing you probably remember is the headline telling you that a baseball went through his legs and cost the Red Sox a clinching win in Game 6 of the 1986 World Series. What that one unfortunate incident drowned out is the fact that Buckner had a very good Major League Baseball career, amassing more than 2,700 hits and 1,200 RBI in 20-plus years as a pro. How does this relate to Carter? Easy.

If you mention Jimmy Carter and *sports* to the average adult who was alive during his presidency, they'll likely bring up the time he collapsed during a 10k race at the Catoctin Mountain Park Run in Maryland. The race took place at a critical juncture in his presidency, when the polls were down and the political heat was turned way up. But despite the difficulty of the race (lots of hills), Carter was ready to go and there was no reason for anyone to be concerned. After all, he had been a member of the Naval Academy's cross country team, and he'd been running 40 to 50 miles per week in preparation for the race.

"I start looking forward to it [running] almost from the minute I get up," Carter told the *New York Times* at the time. "If I don't run, I don't feel exactly right. I carry a watch, and I can click off a mile in 6½ minutes when I really turn it on."

On race day, Carter never got to turn it on; or perhaps he turned it on too much, too early. Whatever the reason, whether it was the steep hills or the 90-degree temperatures, about three-and-a-half miles into the race the president bonked out and collapsed into the arms of a Secret Service agent who had been running behind him.

Most people feared that the president had suffered a heart attack, but in the end his doctor said it was just heat exhaustion, and Carter was escorted to the finish line in time to hand out trophies to the winners. But while his physical recovery was swift, his athletic reputation suffered lasting repercussions, as the "running collapse" overshadowed what was otherwise a very active, athletic life.

Carter played on his high school's tennis and basketball teams, and was a pole vaulter on the track team. He also played American Legion baseball.

As president, Carter played tennis five times a week and was even in charge of the schedule for the courts on the White House property. When given the opportunity, he also played golf, ran, and hiked in the woods while on vacation. Post-presidency, Carter took up downhill skiing, hiked Mount Kilimanjaro, picked up swimming, and continued to run until he was about 80 and his knees gave out. He is the longest-living president we've ever had, and he credits his health and longevity to constant exercise and a healthy diet, despite admitting to *Time* magazine that he didn't consider himself a good athlete.

As far as presidents go, we beg to differ.

WhAR (White House Athlete Ranking)

Executive Power

Jimmy Carter is clearly one of our most active presidents, but nearly all of his activities fall on the "fitness" side of things rather than the "strength" side of things. At 5-foot-9 and 160 pounds, Carter is on the slighter side of the POTUS power curve.

SCORE: 4

Running Ability

Cross-country running. Baseball. Tennis. Basketball. Track. You name it, and if it was non-contact, Carter did it. This category is all about a president's level of commitment to sports before taking office, and on that note, Carter is at the top of the list.

SCORE: 8

Fit for Office

Organizing the White House tennis matches is a notch on his Fit for Office belt. Training for and running a 10k (despite the outcome) is another. Kudos to Carter for playing as many sports in office as he had prior to his election.

SCORE: 7

Executive Achievement

Participation in a lot of sports is the way to a high score in the previous category. A slew of defining athletic moments is the path to a 10 here. Carter doesn't have a marathon or college title to brag about, but for him we're going to take more of a lifetime achievement approach. After all, who wouldn't trade a trophy won at 18 or 20 years old to be running into your 80s and swimming into your mid-90s?

SCORE: 10

Mettle of Honor:

None of the sports that Carter was passionate about are

particularly grueling on a weekend warrior level. There's nothing wrong with that, but this category measures athletic mettle and there aren't many places to find points for him here.

SCORE: 5

WhAR: 34

OVERALL RANKING: #12

James Garfield

HEIGHT: 6'
WEIGHT: 180
COLLEGE: Williams College
SPORTS: Fishing, Brawling, Military

PRESIDENT JAMES GARFIELD had brawler's blood. His dad Abram Garfield built a reputation as a wrestler, a strongman, and a tough guy not to be trifled with. The best description of Abram is from Capt. Amos Letcher of the Evening Star, a canal boat on the Ohio River. Letcher gave a young James Garfield a job on his boat as a canal hand, and soon after leaving the dock on his first voyage the crew tested the future president. They picked on him and bullied him, and for a short time he refused to fight back. I'll let Capt. Letcher take it from here.

"Next morning, one of the hands accused Jim of being a coward because he would not fight for his rights," Letcher described in *The Life of James Abram Garfield*. Then he told his crew, "Jim may be a coward for aught I know, but if he is, he is the first one of the name I ever knew that was. His father was no coward. He helped dig this canal, and weighed over two hundred pounds, and could take a barrel of whiskey by the chime and drink out of the bunghole and no man dared call him a coward. You'll alter your mind about Jim, before fall."

I don't know what "taking a barrel of whiskey in the chime" is or how impressed I should be about drinking out of the bunghole, but what I do know is that the crew didn't have to wait until the fall to find out what Garfield was made of.

According to William Ralston Balch, the author of *The Life of James Abram Garfield,* the next day, Garfield's "setting pole" slipped from his hand when the boat unexpectedly lunged, and it hit one of his crewmates named Dave. Dave became "furiously enraged and threatened to thrash the offender within an inch of his life, and with his head down, rushed like a mad bull at Garfield."

Garfield remained "quietly confident," side-stepped Dave, and just as he was about to be tackled delivered a crushing right hook, crumpling the man to the ground. Garfield jumped on top of Dave and was about to pummel him, but realized Dave was helpless and let him up. The two shook hands and became fast friends.

"This fight was, however, preliminary to many others during his three months on the two paths," Balch wrote. "As the boys on the canal [continued to bully him] it was constantly necessary [for James] to remind them that he wouldn't be bullied, which he always did most effectually by the virtue of his toughened muscles."

Garfield's toughened muscles (and brilliant mind) would come in to play a few years later while he was working his way up to brigadier general in the Civil War. During the Battle of Middle Creek, a 29-year-old Garfield found himself outnumbered two-to-one against a Confederate position. Rather than retreat, he tricked the Confederates into thinking he had greater numbers and then attacked, forcing a five-hour-long battle of hand-to-hand combat — which he won.

Later in the war, Garfield's legend of toughness and grit would grow when he almost single-handedly took over a steamer on the Ohio River. After every boat pilot refused to navigate the dangerous channels, he took the helm for roughly 48 hours straight and got the boat full of supplies and his men where they needed to go.

When he wasn't laying the smackdown on bullies, facing overwhelming odds in battle, or taking control of an impossible situation, Garfield also enjoyed hunting, fishing and billiards in his free time.

Sadly, Garfield was assassinated just over six months after being elected president.

WhAR (White House Athlete Ranking)

Executive Power

When your dad is the late 1700s version of "Stone Cold" Steve Austin and you have a penchant for pounding people with your fists when they test you as a young man, it's safe to say you come from hearty stock. Garfield is our first president to rise above generalities like "big guy strength" and earn an *actual* high score in the strength department — no doubt making Big Abram Garfield proud. Let's all chime some whiskey to celebrate our first 10 here.

SCORE: 10

Running Ability

James Garfield had no time for fitness or exercise while he was in his late 20s and early 30s because he was too busy crushing Confederate forces and showing his men what hand-to-hand combat was all about.

SCORE: 6

Fit for Office

Garfield was only in office for six months, so this is the one area where we can't give him a high score.

SCORE: 2

Executive Achievement

When Garfield was only 10 or 12 he wanted to earn some money, so he committed to delivering 100 cords of wood to a local businessman for $25. He had never chopped wood before, and the axe was a quarter of his body weight, and it was an insane task to tackle. And yet, after two full days of blistered hands and sore shoulders, he delivered the wood and earned his money. And that's not even one of his coolest tough-guy achievements, as we've covered.

SCORE: 7

Mettle of Honor:

In terms of activities that will earn you a high score in the mettle department, hand-to-hand combat, repeatedly winning fights on a boat against men twice your age, and taking over a ship in a torrential downpour for two straight days will get you a 10 every time.

SCORE: 10

WhAR: 35

OVERALL RANKING: #11

CHAPTER 6:
SULTANS OF THE SMITHSONIAN

These presidents were into exercising their bodies as much as they were into exercising power.

Barack Obama

HEIGHT: 6'1½"
WEIGHT: 180
COLLEGE: Harvard
SPORTS: Basketball, Golf

AS A MODERN president, Barack Obama poses a true test for the WhAR system. On one hand, his love for basketball and golf is well documented, he has a decent jump shot (despite playing in sweatpants sometimes), and he was dedicated to hitting the gym regularly while in office, which we'll get to later. On the other hand, he has thrown some truly pitiful first pitches and demonstrated clown-like bowling ability. Up to this point, we haven't really sliced and diced between what counts as "staying in shape" versus what is actual athletic ability, but as we get into the top 10 of our list, these distinctions matter and we have to start taking into account true athleticism displayed across a variety of sports and activities. This is even more important for the presidents of the last 50 years or so because all of their skills (or lack thereof) have been preserved on video for all to see.

When it comes to Obama's case for ascending to the top of the athletic pyramid for presidential athletes, let's start with the good:

He is by far the best basketball player we've ever had in the Oval Office. His love for the game began as a kid and only intensified in his teens, as he played pick-up hoops every day on an outdoor court at school. When he attended Hawaii's Punahou High School, the left-handed small forward was a member of the junior varsity and varsity squads and won a state championship in 1979. Although Obama wasn't in the starting five, his teammate Mark Bendix told NBC News, "he had a pretty good shot and really handled the ball well."

After high school, Obama attended Occidental College, and this is where things get a little murky. According to some accounts, he was an actual member of the school basketball team. According to others, he just played a ton of pick-up games with the actual guys on the team. The *Los Angeles Times* did a deep dive on this and could not find a single photo, box score, or mention in the school paper of Obama on the team. But one of the coaches, Mike Zinn, swears that he did play, even though some players don't know for sure.

"He was really athletic, ran good, jumped good," Zinn said in the *L.A. Times* piece. "He wasn't a great outside shooter. In basketball terminology, he was kind of a slasher. He was left-handed. He went left well, didn't go right that well."

In that same *L.A. Times* article, it's stated that in Obama's 1995 autobiography *"Dreams from My Father,"* Obama wrote that he played basketball "with a consuming passion that would always exceed my limited talent," but makes no mention of playing at Occidental.

Regardless of whether he was on the roster or not, it's clear that Obama played hoops as much as he could during his time on campus.

Years later when Obama was running for office, it seemed that nearly every campaign stop featured a shoot-around or a quick pick-up game. He even famously played games on Election Day. The verdict: the 44th president was an above average pick-up player in his heyday who could hold his own with better athletes and often rose to the occasion on the court.

The other sport Obama is most associated with is golf. Even though he didn't play much before he took office, he quickly made up for lost time by logging 306 rounds over eight years, or roughly 38 rounds a year, which is well above the 19 rounds a year the average golfer plays, according to the National Golf Foundation.

By his own admission, he hits a decent driver but can get caught in sand traps. During a *Morning Drive* interview on the Golf Channel, Obama estimated that he's about a 13 handicap and typically scores in the low to mid-80s, which isn't bad at all.

Aside from basketball and golf, Obama made exercise a priority while in office, working out as much as six days a week and rotating between cardio and circuit training in the White House gym first thing in the morning.

"Most of my workouts have to come before my day starts," he told *Men's Health* in an interview. "There's always a trade-off between sleep and working out. Usually I get in about 45 minutes, six days a week. I'll lift one day, do cardio the next. I wish I was getting a 90-minute workout."

Thus far, we've built a stellar case for Obama to be one of the most athletic presidents we've ever had — and he is — but we're entering rarified air and we have to mention a few of the negatives.

All you have to do is google "Obama first pitch" and you'll find a few videos you won't soon forget. But Obama didn't grow up playing baseball, so it's hard to knock him too much for that one. There are also a few photos and videos out there of Obama playing beach football, a la Johnny Utah. It's hard to decipher whether these images help or hurt his case, but the fact that he's playing and running around certainly helps. And I'm not here to argue whether or not bowling is a sport, but it's a decent indication of hand-eye coordination, and even mildly athletic middle school kids can break 75. Obama is on record with a 37.

WhAR (White House Athlete Ranking)

Executive Power

Obama is definitely on the trim side in terms of his build, but his commitment to weight training while in office scores him major points here. While he's not a powerful guy like Teddy Roosevelt or Ford or Lincoln, he's clearly not a pushover either.

SCORE: 7

Running Ability

A lifetime of running pick-up hoops games will account for a bulk of Obama's score here, and his overall activity level and love of sports pushes him above most other POTUSes.

SCORE: 9

Fit for Office

Regular pick-up hoops games. Cardio three days a week. Weight training three days a week. Nearly 40 rounds of golf a year. If you didn't know that Obama accomplished that while he was president, you might think he was retired.

SCORE: 10

Executive Achievement

Obama doesn't have one signature moment to call his own in the achievement category. He was a member of a high school state championship team but didn't start. He either was or wasn't on the freshman hoops team at Occidental College. What I'm going to do is give him a lifetime achievement award for four decades of pick-up basketball and 300-plus rounds of golf in eight years.

SCORE: 8

Mettle of Honor:

This is the one category in which our 44th president will not be among the elite. He didn't serve in the military, so he has no active duty. He didn't play football or box or wrestle or play any of our more physical sports. And he doesn't have a marathon or other tough endurance event to his credit. When historians look upon rankings and wonder why Obama wasn't among the top 5 most athletic presidents, his score in this category will be the reason.

SCORE: 5

WhAR: 39

OVERALL RANKING: #10

Ronald Reagan

HEIGHT: 6'1"
WEIGHT: 185
COLLEGE: Eureka College
SPORTS: Swimming, Football, Basketball, Track

SEVENTY-SEVEN.

That's the number of lives Ronald Reagan saved over seven summers as a lifeguard at Lowell Park Beach, earning him the nickname Reaganhoff (okay, maybe I'm the only one who calls him that, but this is my book so you're just going to have to get on board the Reaganhoff train). Point in fact, to this day there is a bronze plaque at the beach commemorating Reagan's service. There is even a push to get a bronze statue built there in his honor.

When Reagan wasn't saving lives in the lake he was winning medals in the pool. In high school, his crawl (freestyle) was unbeatable and his prowess in the water earned him a full scholarship to Eureka College (where he also played football). Once at Eureka, he went undefeated in the pool his freshman year. Through a series of odd events, Reagan actually took over as the team's coach the following season and remained a swimmer/coach for the rest of his time in college. His feats in the pool and in the lake were eventually recognized by the International Swimming Hall of Fame when they made him a recipient of their Gold Medallion award in 1988.

On dry land, Reagan played football, basketball and ran track at Dixon High School, and then continued to play football at Eureka, as I mentioned. While Reagan's actual athletic exploits were cause for recognition (even at a small school like Eureka), it's perhaps his fictional portrayal of George "The Gipper" Gipp in the film *Knute Rockne: All American* that he's best known for, athletically speaking.

Following a long career as an actor and a politician in California, Reagan was (at the time) the oldest man to be elected president, taking office at the age of 73. And yet, exercise and sports remained a priority for the septuagenarian.

In a *PARADE* magazine article in 1983, Reagan wrote a story called "How to Stay Fit." In the piece, the Gipper extolled the virtues of swimming, body surfing, horseback riding, and the "hard manual labor" of cutting, stacking and hauling wood outside. In the second part of the feature, he talked specifically about his training routine in the small White House gym (remember this was the early 1980s).

"Our little gym is equipped with a weight scale, exercycle, treadmill, a leg-lift contraption, and a machine with pulleys and weights that enables me to do a variety of exercises for arms, stomach, shoulders and legs. There is also a rack of handweights, which sort of looks like a xylophone, with weights of up to 15 pounds a piece," he wrote.

Reagan typically hit the gym at night and described his program as, "10 minutes of warm-up calisthenics, aimed at limbering up specific muscles, followed by about 15 minutes of workout on the machines."

"I have two different sets of exercises I do on alternate days," he wrote. "Each exercise is for specific muscles. The specific exercises are not any different than you could find in many of the fitness centers that have opened all over the country — bench presses, leg lifts and the like."

WhAR (White House Athlete Ranking)

Executive Power

Reagan was a strong swimmer, football player and horseback rider, but he was not overall one of our more physically powerful presidents. He gets credit for playing football, but Eureka College was a very small school, so he likely wasn't a physical specimen. His overall fitness level certainly places him above average, but since we're in the cream of the crop of POTUS athletes, Reagan won't reach the top rung in this category.

SCORE: 7

Running Ability

Sports and fitness were clear priorities for Ronald Reagan throughout his life, though he actually preferred to work on his ranch building fences, chopping wood and putting in a hard day's work outside. Major bonus points for getting his hands dirty the old-fashioned way while also adopting circuit training and other more modern forms of exercise.

SCORE: 10

Fit for Office

We have to take into account that Reagan was 73 when he took office, so he was well past his days of taking up mountain biking like Bush 43 or playing regular pick-up hoops like Obama. But on the flip side, we have to give a man that age credit for hitting the gym and the pool as often as he did. In a version of what Reagan famously told Walter Mondale during a debate, we won't hold his age and experience against him.

SCORE: 9

Executive Achievement

In my estimation, it's a tie between the 77 lifeguard saves and the undefeated freshman swimming season for Reagan's most athletic achievement. If the undefeated year in the pool were at a swimming powerhouse like UCLA or Texas, I'd give it a higher score, but since it's at a smaller school, I have to drop him a bit.

SCORE: 7

Mettle of Honor:

Reagan served in the military, but due to an eyesight issue he never fought overseas. He gets a few points for playing football (even at a small school), a few more for his lumberjacking ways on his ranch, and a couple more for dragging nearly seven dozen people out of the water and preventing them from drowning.

SCORE: 7

WhAR: 40

OVERALL RANKING: #9

Dwight Eisenhower

HEIGHT: 5'10½"
WEIGHT: 180
COLLEGE: West Point
SPORTS: Football, Golf, Baseball

BEFORE PRESIDENT DWIGHT Eisenhower was known to the world as "Ike," he had already earned an excellent sports nickname on the gridiron: the Kansas Cyclone. The name was given to him when he was a high school football star in Abilene, Kansas. As a running back and punishing linebacker, the future president earned a local reputation for seemingly being everywhere on the field at once, wreaking havoc on the other team at will. A local sportswriter labeled him "the Kansas Cyclone" in his coverage and the phenomenal nickname stuck.

As good as he was as an individual talent in football, his first taste of true team success was with Abilene High School's baseball team, for which he played center field during the team's undefeated season in 1909.

After high school, his skills as an athlete helped him earn a scholarship to West Point, where he'd become a star on the team and be part of one of the most legendary games in the history of college football.

The star for Carlisle was the legend himself, Jim Thorpe. Prior to the match-up against West Point, Thorpe had recently won a host of gold medals at the Stockholm Olympics, and the King of Sweden called him the greatest athlete in the world.

Heading into the game, the West Point players formed a game plan that centered on stopping Thorpe. In the book *Carlisle vs. Army,* author Lars Anderson wrote, "A cadet would become famous, the Army players believed, if he knocked Thorpe out of the game with a hit so powerful it kidnapped Thorpe from consciousness."

Eisenhower, as the team's featured linebacker, firmly believed that he was going to be the one to take out Thorpe — and as fate would have it, he was right. Early in the game, Eisenhower and another teammate found themselves face to face with the oncoming bowling ball that was Thorpe, and they dropped their shoulders to lower the boom on the Olympic champion. Thorpe fumbled the ball and squirmed on the ground in pain while the Kansas Cyclone celebrated.

The celebration would be short lived, however, as Thorpe recovered and re-entered the game. After his return, Eisenhower and a fellow linebacker once again had Thorpe in their sights and aimed to deliver what they thought would be the blow to knock him out of the game. At the last second, Thorpe sidestepped both blockers and Eisenhower slammed into his teammate and broke his leg, effectively ending his football career. Carlisle won the game 27–6, snapping Army's winning streak.

Following his time at West Point, Eisenhower was promoted to Captain just after the United States entered World War I. At that point he became a career soldier, working his way up from commanding a single post to the Supreme Allied Commander in Europe. He became Chief of Staff of the United States Army over several decades before he would eventually be elected president following victory in World War II.

Though Eisenhower would coach various football teams during his career, the sport he was by far the most passionate about was golf. He played more than 800 rounds while in office, and even had a putting green installed on the White House grounds. According to a feature in *Golf Week*, after a long day, it was common to see

Ike throw on his cleats, grab a wedge, an 8-iron and a putter and head to the south lawn for some practice.

His handicap fluctuated between 14 and 18. The course he is most associated with is none other than the home of the Masters in Augusta, Georgia. As if Eisenhower was trying to establish a tradition unlike any other, he played Augusta 29 times during his two terms in office, and has a tree named after him (the Eisenhower Tree) on the 17th hole. The *Golf Week* article states that Eisenhower broke 80 four times in his life at the famous course, but it would have been more if it wasn't for that tree, which he could never seem to figure out on his approach to the green. He even lobbied to have it removed.

The 34th president counted Arnold Palmer among his closest friends and playing partners, and he was eventually elected to the World Golf Hall of Fame in the Lifetime Achievement category.

WhAR (White House Athlete Ranking)

Executive Power

Dwight Eisenhower was never a physically intimidating presence, but in his day, he was a hard-hitting linebacker who liked to get his nose dirty. He gets points for excelling at a tough position in football (especially with the flimsy pads and helmets of his day), but he's not among the group of our strongest presidents.

SCORE: 7.5

Running Ability

The knee injury Eisenhower suffered during the West Point game against Jim Thorpe affected him for quite some time, and he never played team sports at a high level again. Since he was a career soldier he always stayed in trim shape, but other than golf, Ike didn't have much time for other exercise.

SCORE: 7

Fit for Office

This entire score comes down to how much you value golf as a sport and where you rank it in terms of requiring athletic ability rather than hand-eye coordination and nerves. I am going to rank Ike slightly above average here, giving him a score ahead of all of the "walking presidents" but below some of our more committed Oval Office athletes.

SCORE: 7

Executive Achievement

Going undefeated in any sport at any level is great, so kudos to Eisenhower for being a part of his undefeated baseball squad in high school. He also had a starring role on what was then considered the best football team in the country at West Point, so he's got that going for him as well. And breaking 80 at Augusta is every golfer's dream. Add it up and Eisenhower is near the top of the class in terms of executive athletic achievement.

SCORE: 9

Mettle of Honor

Eisenhower thrived in one of the toughest sports we have during its absolute toughest time to be a player. He also oversaw D-Day and effectively helped save the world against Hitler and Germany. So.... 10.

SCORE: 10

WhAR: 40.5

OVERALL RANKING: #8

John F. Kennedy

HEIGHT: 6'
WEIGHT: 175
COLLEGE: Harvard
SPORTS: Swimming, Football, Golf, Tennis, Basketball

JOHN F. KENNEDY would probably rank a little higher on this list if he hadn't suffered from chronic back pain. Like Gale Sayers and Bo Jackson after him, we'll never know exactly what his football career — or his athletic career in general — would've been had he not been injured. Then again, to paraphrase a famous line that Lloyd Bentsen used against Dan Quayle: Sorry Jack, I've watched Bo Jackson and I've studied Bo Jackson, and you're no Bo Jackson (yes, this is a bit of a stretch, but if you bring up Kennedy's name to a certain generation, they claim that he was an outstanding athlete).

So let's start with the facts: JFK was a decent athlete, and in some sports a good athlete, but he wasn't outstanding in any of them.

Kennedy played left end and tackle on the Choate Hall football team (his prep school) before joining Harvard University's squad as a freshman. Harvard's website features a 1970 interview with James Farrell, who was the football trainer during Kennedy's year on the team. Farrell doesn't exactly paint a picture of an overpowering Adonis when discussing Kennedy.

"When Jack arrived on the scene, he didn't look much like an athlete," Farrell said in the interview. "He was a big, tall string bean. You could blow him over with a good breath... As far as his football ability was concerned, he didn't have much physique to play that particular game..."

Ouch.

No matter. Swimming was considered his best sport anyway.

The swim coach probably has something great to say about him, right?

"His physique wasn't anything outstanding," Harvard's long-time swim coach Harold Ulen explained. "As an undergraduate at Harvard, he was rather frail, as I remember."

Double ouch.

Ulen had Kennedy focus on the backstroke and said that he held his own with the other members of the team in that stroke, but "he didn't break any records."

On the bright side, Kennedy saved his most amazing swimming feat for several years later, during World War II when he became a bona fide war hero. After the patrol boat he was commanding in the Pacific theater was rammed by a Japanese Destroyer, the future president dragged shipmate Patrick McMahon more than 3.5 miles through the ocean to safety using a makeshift rope held in his teeth. If that wasn't enough, while the rest of his crew was marooned on an island, Kennedy swam the shipping lanes every day, hoping to flag down a boat to rescue them. He fought brutal currents, fended off coral and often found himself treading water for hours at a time during his attempts to be rescued, which eventually paid off.

In my opinion, those efforts outweigh how he performed against Ivy League backstrokers in the pool.

Beyond football and swimming, Kennedy also played tennis and basketball, and by most accounts would have been an excellent golfer if not for his lower back issues.

"He had a wonderfully lyric swing," author Curt Smith said in an interview on History.com. "I remember talking to a golf pro who told me that if Kennedy had been healthy and had wanted to, he could have been a professional golfer."

WhAR (White House Athlete Ranking)

Executive Power

For me, this score comes down to that heroic swim in which he dragged a crewmate by a rope with his teeth for nearly four miles. It may not be the same raw physical strength that other presidents have displayed, but it's up there. Clearly, Kennedy had a well of power within him that he could summon when he needed it most.

SCORE: 8

Running Ability

This is a difficult category to measure because, while JFK clearly enjoyed sports and an athlete's lifestyle, he was hampered by a host of injuries and likely was as active as his body would let him be for much of his life.

SCORE: 7

Fit for Office

This category has the same dilemma as the previous one. Kennedy was in constant pain while in office, so much so that he wore a back brace and had issues standing at times. It's tough to ding him for that, but this category measures how fit he stayed in office, and his health prevented him from really thriving here.

SCORE: 6

Executive Achievement

The famous rescue swim is all you need to know here. The icing on top is swimming and playing football at Harvard, even if his career was brief and he wasn't that good. Let's focus on the swim. This category is all about that one defining athletic moment, and JFK's tops most.

SCORE: 10

Mettle of Honor:

Another 10. What more could you ask for in a display of both grit and courage than dragging an injured soldier through the water in hostile territory during wartime?

SCORE: 10

WhAR: 41

OVERALL RANKING: #7

George W. Bush

HEIGHT: 6'1"
WEIGHT: 195
COLLEGE: Yale
SPORTS: Running, Weight Lifting, Golf, Baseball

IF PRESIDENTS LITERALLY *ran* for office, George W. Bush would win by a landslide against any of his predecessors. He has appeared on the cover of *Runner's World*, he completed the 1993 Houston Marathon in 3 hours and 44 minutes (as a 46-year-old), and he even had a treadmill installed on Air Force One so he could get his runner's high at 35,000 feet. As president, he once completed a three-mile race in 20 minutes and 20 seconds, which put him on a sub-seven-minute mile pace — not bad for the then 55-year-old.

In a *Wall Street Journal* article, former Secret Service agent Dan Emmett described Bush as "not a jogger but an honest-to-God runner," explaining that very few Secret Service agents could hang with him on a run, despite many of them being much younger than the president. When asked by *Runner's World* about his love for the sport and why he often ran as many as six times a week, he gave this answer:

"First, it helps me sleep at night. Second, it keeps me disciplined. Running also breaks up my day and allows me to recharge my batteries. Running also enables me to set goals and push myself toward those goals. In essence, it keeps me young. A good run adds a little bounce to my step. I get a certain amount of self-esteem from it. Plus, I just look and feel better."

Well said.

After running, Bush took up mountain biking and famously toured the Olympic Course in Beijing before the competition began in 2008. As an ex-president, he started the W100k, a "high-endurance mountain bike ride highlighting the bravery and sacrifice of our nation's warriors."

Like Obama, Bush 43 also hit the White House gym almost daily, doing circuit work as well as free weights. His crowning achievement in the POTUS iron paradise has to be his bench press. At the end of one of his clangin' and bangin' sessions, his trainer reported that Bush jacked up 185 pounds for five reps. And since we have the internet to help us obsess over everything, a Bodybuilding.com message board quickly plugged those numbers into the "projected bench press" chart to determine that Bush's likely max bench was in the 215-pound range — an impressive number for a man in his mid-50s who weighs about 185 pounds.

Also like Obama, Bush played a decent amount of golf when he entered office (he gave it up after 9/11). But unlike Obama, he was considered to be really good. During an interview with *Golf Digest*, Bush admitted that when he played a lot his handicap was in the single digits, which puts him in the upper echelon of amateur golfers.

If you're keeping track, Bush is a well-above-average runner and golfer and an avid mountain biker. He was also stronger in the weight room than a vast majority of men his age, and if you add this stuff up, it clearly puts him near the top of the list — with the marathon and the bench, perhaps a notch above some of the other elite athletes who have occupied the Oval Office.

As we'll get to in a bit, George H.W. Bush was a legitimately excellent college baseball player. W? Not so much. He did make the Yale University squad as a freshman relief pitcher, but he only got into a few games. This experience would, however, prepare him for the most important first pitch ever thrown out in Major League Baseball: the one he threw out at Yankee Stadium after

9/11, which was an honest-to-goodness fastball for a strike with the whole world watching.

After his freshman year of baseball, W ditched the school teams and stuck with intramurals from then on. One little-known fact about Bush is that he was a cheerleader in high school at Philips Academy, and also at Yale. This wasn't exactly cheering of the *Bring it On* variety, but it was cheering nonetheless.

WhAR (White House Athlete Ranking)

Executive Power

There is a big difference between "weight room strength" and real-world brawn, so while Bush scores very well here, he's a few points shy of a 10, which is reserved for the few presidents with feats of strength and power to their name.

SCORE: 8

Running Ability

George W. Bush is the best running president we've ever had. Period.

SCORE: 10

Fit for Office

Bush's commitment to sports and exercise throughout his presidency was perhaps only rivaled by Obama, Roosevelt (as you'll see) and a few other chief executives. Gotta give him the top score here.

SCORE: 10

Executive Achievement

Completing a marathon in under four hours is a tremendous achievement, but now that we're in rarified air, we have to measure that feat against those of other presidents who won national titles and were true blue college athletes or champions. Still, Bush is in the top 5 percent here for sure.

SCORE: 9

Mettle of Honor:

Bush has no military experience to pump up his score here, but he does have the marathon and some serious mountain biking courses to his credit.

SCORE: 5

WhAR: 42

OVERALL RANKING: #6

Abraham Lincoln

HEIGHT: 6'4"
WEIGHT: 190
COLLEGE: none
SPORTS: Handball, Street Fighting, Wrestling

DURING A SCENE in the movie *Fight Club*, Brad Pitt says that if he could fight anybody in history, he'd fight Abraham Lincoln because he was a big guy with a big reach. "Skinny guys fight till they're burger," he says. That may be true, but Tyler Durden, Pitt's character, needs to brush up on his history, because in the Illinois Rail Splitter's younger days, he could've been known as the Illinois Jaw Splitter for his street fighting and wrestling prowess.

The most famous story involving Lincoln busting heads took place in the 1830s, when Lincoln's boss at the general store bet the owner of a bar $10 (nearly $300 today) that young Abe could whip a champion fighter by the name of Jack Armstrong from a few towns over. By this time, Lincoln had established himself as a solid wrestler and was well known for his raw power despite his tall, lean frame.

Nowadays, a fight of this magnitude might take place at Mandalay Bay or Madison Square Garden (I'm kidding), but back then, the town square would do. Hundreds of people came from miles around, odds were laid, and an untold number of bets were placed on the fight. Armstrong, despite being shorter, was far more muscular than Lincoln, was the champion of the region, and was the more experienced fighter.

No matter.

Lincoln fought off the more compact fighter, keeping him at bay with his long arms and surprising horsepower. One witness went on record as saying that Lincoln lifted Armstrong off the ground in the middle of the fight and shook him like a little boy. Eventually, after toying with Armstrong long enough, Lincoln summoned his inner Undertaker, slammed his opponent to the ground, and pinned his shoulders down.

Armstrong's friends were furious and tried to have a go at the victor, but Armstrong himself intervened and shook hands with Lincoln, acknowledging that he was beaten by the superior fighter.

According to a write-up on the National Wrestling Hall of Fame's website, as a wrestler, "Lincoln progressed rapidly between the ages of 19, when he defended his stepbrother's river barge from Natchez thugs, throwing the potential hijackers overboard, and 29, when he cautiously mentioned himself as possibly the second best wrestler in southern Illinois. Lincoln certainly did not achieve any national fame as a wrestler, but his career was typical of the way the sport was conducted in the first half of the 19th century."

The NWHOF's site goes on to describe his fighting discipline as the free-for-all style of the frontier known as "catch as catch can," which was more hand-to-hand combat than sport. He was also a physical specimen, standing at 6-foot-4 with loads of natural lean muscle from hard work on the edges of civilization. The site's piece on Lincoln concludes that he was undoubtedly the roughest and toughest of the wrestling presidents.

When he wasn't embarrassing tough guys or ending slavery, Lincoln was an avid handball player. In fact, the Smithsonian still has his lucky ball.

WhAR (White House Athlete Ranking)

Executive Power

Standing at 6-foot-4 and cut with lean muscle from hard days in the field, Lincoln was the picture of raw strength.

SCORE: 10

Running Ability

Lincoln wrestled throughout his teens as a local champion, and well into his early 30s. He has only one recorded wrestling loss in that time, which means he must have stayed in top shape to take on all comers for well over a decade.

SCORE: 8

Fit for Office

Lincoln can be forgiven for not dedicating as much time to his physical health as some other presidents. He was dealing with the greatest crisis the nation had known since its inception, the Civil War. Still, Lincoln played plenty of handball right up until his run for office, and even played when the delegates in Chicago were voting on whether he'd be the Republican nominee for president. "For such an awkward fellow," he is quoted as saying after his re-election, "I am pretty sure-footed. It used to take a pretty dexterous man to throw me."

SCORE: 6

Executive Achievement

As we've noted, Lincoln was a wrestling champion, but he also had the smack talking to go along with it. According to an article on Fightland.com, "after one particular scrap where he [Lincoln] defeated a man with a single toss, Abe turned to the angry mob that had gathered to watch the fight, and challenged the lot of them by loudly declaring, 'Any of you want to try it, come on and whet your horns!'"

SCORE: 9

Mettle of Honor:

Being a champion at hand-to-hand combat on the American frontier in the 1800s has to be among the very definitions of mettle.

SCORE: 10

WhAR: 43

OVERALL RANKING: #5

CHAPTER 5:
MOUNT RUSHMORE – THE ATHLETES

Of the seven or eight true jocks elected to the White House, these four men excelled in one sport and were excellent at many others — the sign of a true athlete. Amid all the political jockeying in Washington D.C., these presidents were both politicians and jocks.

.

George H. W. Bush

HEIGHT: 6'2"
WEIGHT: 190
COLLEGE: Yale
SPORTS: Baseball, Tennis, Golf, Fishing

HE PLAYED GOLF with Tiger Woods. He played tennis with Anna Kournikova. He celebrated his 80th, 85th and 90th birthdays by skydiving. He caught a 135-pound tarpon off the coast of the Florida Keys. Prior to George H.W. Bush's passing at the age of 94, he was without question the fittest octogenarian ex-president the United States had ever seen.

"Sports are good for the soul, good for life," he told Monte Burke in an interview with *Forbes*.

If ever there was a mantra that our 41st president lived by, this was it.

As a high school student at Andover Prep School, Bush was captain of the baseball and soccer teams, playing first base on the former and center forward on the latter. After that, he took his talents to New Haven, Connecticut, where he continued to play soccer and baseball, but dropped soccer after his freshman year at Yale to focus on America's pastime, which was also his one true sporting love.

Bush was an elite-fielding first baseman for the Bulldogs who hit righty and threw lefty. The Society for Baseball Research has on record that over the course of his college career, he appeared in 76 games, hit .224 with 13 doubles, a triple, a home run and 28 RBI. In the field, where he excelled, his numbers are much better. He committed only 12 errors during his entire time in college, giving him a solid .983 fielding percentage.

The highlight of his playing days was undoubtedly his

back-to-back appearances in the College World Series in 1947 and 1948. The 1947 series was actually the very first NCAA-sanctioned College World Series tournament to determine a national champion. Yale beat Clemson and then New York University to win the Eastern Playoff division, and went on to face California, the Western Division champ, in the finals. Unfortunately, they'd lose the best-of-three series in two straight games, including a 17-4 loss in the first game.

In 1948 they made the finals again, but lost to the University of Southern California.

Bush would maintain a love of baseball for the rest of his life, using his political connections to hang with guys like Ted Williams and Joe DiMaggio, as well as throw out dozens of first pitches at stadiums across the country. And let's not forget that he kept his first baseman's mitt from Yale in his desk drawer in the Oval Office.

While in the White House, both as Reagan's vice president and as the president himself, he played tennis regularly with staffers — and with 18-time Grand Slam champion Chris Evert.

"He had this killer instinct on the court and off," Evert once said. "He wanted to win at everything. Even Scrabble."

Bush's love of tennis even affected the state of the free world for about 10 minutes. How?

When Ronald Reagan was president, he had to go under anesthesia for colon surgery. While he was out of commission, Bush was the de facto president. The procedure for Reagan lasted eight hours, and during that time Bush decided to play a few games of tennis. While he was playing, he tripped and whacked his head on the ground, knocking him briefly unconscious. There weren't many people around to witness it, but for about five to 10 minutes, Reagan and Bush were both out cold and Tip O'Neill was president of the United States.

H.W.'s third (or fourth, or fifth?) love was golf, which he often bent to his will by playing a form of speed-golf, allowing him to blast through rounds in under two hours. Of course, he also played with Arnold Palmer.

WhAR (White House Athlete Ranking)

Executive Power

This is the one category in determining Bush's WhAR score in which he doesn't reach the mountaintop. He was tall and lean and wasn't overpowering in contact sports or fighting. He also wasn't a power hitter during his glory days in baseball. He was clearly stronger than many of our other presidents, but as we've reached the cream of the crop, his strength doesn't match the power of our strongest POTUSes.

SCORE: 7

Running Ability

We can safely assume that George H.W. Bush began enjoying sports and a physically active lifestyle around age four, which means he spent roughly 90 years as an athlete. He played tennis, golf and baseball his whole life, and even famously showed up to meetings on a bicycle while he was vice president.

SCORE: 9

Fit for Office

During Bush's one term in office, he wasn't as much of a dedicated road runner or cyclist as his son, and he wasn't as committed to the gym as Obama or Reagan, but his activity level remained high despite being much older.

SCORE: 7.5

Executive Achievement

Two College World Series appearances is the second-most impressive organized team sports feat achieved by any of our presidents. That's an automatic 10.

SCORE: 10

Mettle of Honor

The sports that George H.W. Bush enjoyed weren't necessarily known for toughness (tennis, golf, baseball) but he had one of the most dangerous jobs in World War II as a pilot in the Navy, and he survived his plane being shot down in the Pacific, which makes him plenty tough for this category.

SCORE: 10

WhAR: 43.5

OVERALL RANKING: #4

George Washington

HEIGHT: 6'2"
WEIGHT: 220 pounds (estimated)
COLLEGE: none
SPORTS: Horse Riding, Feats of Strength, Early Javelin

ROUGHLY TWO CENTURIES before Bruce Wilhelm and Bill Kazmaier dominated the World's Strongest Man competition for the United States, another soon-to-be American man (because there was no America yet) was performing his own feats of strength that would echo through the ages.

I'm of course talking about George Washington, whose lifelong displays of power put him on par with the tales we've heard about Paul Bunyan.

When Washington was in his 20s, he worked as a surveyor in the untamed woods of the Ohio Valley. As he traipsed through hundreds of miles of wilderness there were no towns, no tools and very few people. It was also freezing, as his work carried him through the winter. No matter. Washington built rafts to travel the Ohio River with nothing but his bare hands and his legendary brawn — pulling trees from the ground, splitting trunks and breaking branches. He also hacked new trails by physically removing the growth in his way — for hundreds of miles.

As a General of the Continental Army, Washington was constantly in the presence of men who looked up to him, both as their leader and physically. The average height for a man in the late 1700s was a shade under 5-foot-8 with a weight of 160 pounds or so. At 6-foot-2 and nearly 220 pounds, Washington towered over his men (and almost all other men of his day). And occasionally, he liked to show off his raw power.

The famous colonial painter Charles Wilson Peale describes

one such moment that took place at Mount Vernon in 1773, when several men visiting his property were competing in a game of "pitching the iron bar," which was basically a javelin contest. But instead of seeing how far they could throw a well-crafted, aerodynamic javelin, men in the 1700s competed to see how far they could chuck a giant heavy metal rod.

Toward the end of the competition, Washington appeared and, while still wearing his coat, reached out his hand for the rod. I'll let Peale explain what happened next.

"No sooner…did that heavy iron bar feel the grasp of his mighty hand than it lost the power of gravitation and whizzed through the air, striking the ground far, very far, beyond our utmost limits," he said.

And if that's not enough, Washington put a little icing on the cake by talking some smack as he admired his throw.

"When you beat my pitch, young gentlemen," he said, "I'll try again."

Chalk one up for POTUS No. 1.

There are plenty of other stories about Washington's rocket launcher of an arm.

His step-grandson George Washington Parke Custis confirmed that he witnessed the General hurl a piece of slate clear across the Rappahonnock River at Fredericksburg — a feat many men had tried but all had failed to do.

Another seemingly impossible challenge that tempted strong-armed men of the area was to throw a rock over the Natural Bridge formation in Rockbridge County, Virginia, which stood 215 feet tall. Of course, Washington was the first (and only) person of his era to do it.

Rest assured, GW didn't use his formidable strength just to break the boundaries of how far or how high he could throw things. At age 18, Washington enrolled in Rev. James Maury's Academy at Fredericksburg, Virginia and began wrestling in the "collar and elbow" style that was popular in his day. In a very short time, Washington became the champion of the academy, then the county, and it's rumored (though not confirmed) that he was the colony champion as well.

His wrestling skills remained throughout his life and he occasionally broke them out to prove a point. When he was 47, a group of Massachusetts Volunteers who had heard about Washington's wrestling skills as a young man were getting a little full of themselves and talked about how they could take the general. Never one to back down from a challenge, Washington, 20 years the men's senior, said he'd take on anyone who thought they were up to it. In an 18th century gauntlet of sorts, Washington laid the smack down and defeated seven consecutive challengers.

He was also a lifelong swimmer, archer and billiards player, but if you asked Americans in the colonies what Washington was best at, they wouldn't have said throwing things or even wrestling. They would have said horseback riding.

No less than Thomas Jefferson said that Washington was "the best horseman of the age." Nearly everyone who saw him on a horse came away with the same impression, stating that he, "rode as he did everything else, with ease, elegance and with power."

WhAR (White House Athlete Ranking)

Executive Power

After examining the evidence and taking into account the lifestyle and era in which he lived, it is safe to say that George Washington was the naturally strongest president we've ever had. If he lived in modern times, there is little doubt he'd be the first president to bench 300 pounds and/or throw a football 80 yards and/or have a 90-mile-an-hour fastball.

SCORE: 10

Running Ability

Washington spent most of his 40s and 50s leading the Continental Army in battle and keeping the ragtag group of revolutionaries together. He didn't have a specific exercise routine, but he rode thousands of miles on his horse, trained his men and likely walked several miles each day inspecting his officers.

SCORE: 8

Fit for Office

Washington was 57 when he took office, which was equivalent to probably 77 today. He maintained his health with daily horse rides. He was also fond of formal dancing at events, which could often last for hours and, though not intense, was a decent form of cardio for an old man.

SCORE: 6

Executive Achievement

Colonial wrestling champion. Iron pitch champion. The first man to ever clear the Natural Bridge with a rock. Yeah, that's a 10.

SCORE: 10

Mettle of Honor

We're going with back-to-back 10s here. It would almost be automatic after winning the Revolutionary War under such dire circumstances, but the wrestling skills, both as a young man and later in life, clinch it.

SCORE: 10

WhAR: 44

OVERALL RANKING: #3

Theodore Roosevelt

HEIGHT: 5'10"
WEIGHT: 180-200 pounds
COLLEGE: Harvard
SPORTS: Boxing, Marital Arts, Hunting, Football, Tennis, Rowing

WHEN IT COMES to sports, fitness, fighting and breaking a sweat, Theodore Roosevelt was without question the most enthusiastic, committed and flat-out craziest president we've ever had. He also enjoyed the widest variety of physical pursuits of any president, with interests ranging from martial arts to football and tennis, rowing, boxing and more. As such, his exploits across these fields are not only the most documented by the press and historians, but by the man himself in his writings, journals and letters. For this reason, I'm taking a slightly deeper dive here to fully appreciate the scope of TR's athleticism and willingness to push himself.

Roosevelt the Wrestler

When most presidents take a beating, they do it in the head-lines, not while in a headlock. Teddy Roosevelt preferred the literal version.

During his political career, he voluntarily subjected himself to a staggering number of sparring sessions with championship-cal-iber fighters. Boxers, wrestlers, martial artists — it didn't matter to Roosevelt. If they were willing to punch him in the face or pin him to the ground, he'd take them on. He felt it was the only way he could maintain his "natural body prowess."

Imagine Barack Obama having Roy Jones Jr. over to the White House gym for some heavy bag work and shadow boxing; or Don-ald Trump rolling around an Oval Office octagon with Brock

Lesnar. That's the level of commitment we're talking about with Roosevelt. And this obsession started long before he was elected president.

While Roosevelt was governor of New York, he discovered that the American middleweight wrestling champion was training in Albany. The instant he heard the news, he summoned the wrestler to the Governor's Mansion. After a short conversation, the wrestler agreed to come over three or four afternoons a week to train him. Roosevelt, who was in his early 40s at the time (nearly double the age of the wrestler), looked forward to his training sessions so much that he bought a wrestling mat for the workout room. While neither combatant had a problem with the wrestling mat, Roosevelt's comptroller did and he refused to audit the bill for the mat, claiming that wrestling wasn't "proper Gubernatorial amusement."

TR the Boxer

Despite not letting the people of New York pay for the wrestling mat, the comptroller felt bad that Roosevelt wouldn't have anybody to spar with when the wrestler had to leave Albany, and he volunteered a friend who was a professional oarsman. During his second training session with the oarsman, Roosevelt caved in the poor guy's ribs and then suffered his own shoulder injury. With both men bloodied and bruised, it was decided that it might not be best for the Governor of New York to look like he was squaring off against Bill the Butcher every other day. Once Roosevelt recovered, he went back to his first love of boxing.

Roosevelt's boxing career began the same way Mike Tyson's did — with an ass-kicking at the hands of bullies. Tyson had a speech impediment. Roosevelt had asthma. Both afflictions made these future pugilists appear weak and ripe for bullying. In Tyson's case, he learned early on that he was born with cinder blocks for fists and that he could punch his way through those who would taunt him. Eventually, the taunting stopped and the cheering began. Roosevelt, on the other hand, wasn't born with a natural ability to fend for himself. In fact, he was born the opposite.

As a child, he was more like Samuel L. Jackson's Mr. Glass in *Unbreakable* than the eventual Rough Rider he would become. Here's how the future president describes himself as a child in his autobiography: "Having been a sickly boy, with no natural bodily prowess ... I was at first quite unable to hold my own when thrown into contact with other boys of rougher antecedents. I was nervous and timid."

And here's how he describes the first real beating he took: "Having an attack of asthma, I was sent off by myself to Moosehead Lake. On the stage-coach ride ... I encountered a couple of other boys who were about my own age ... They found that I was a foreordained and predestined victim, and industriously proceeded to make life miserable for me. The worst feature was that when I finally tried to fight them, I discovered that either singly could not only handle me with easy contempt, but handle me so as not to hurt me and yet to prevent my doing any damage whatever in return."

In short, they toyed with the future president. This incident scarred Roosevelt, and he resolved that day to do something about it. Shortly after returning from his trip, he asked his father's permission to learn how to box. His dad set him up with ex-prizefighter John Long, and from there Roosevelt's love affair with the sweet science began. Roosevelt began his training with little natural ability, but he was eager to learn and practiced hard. After a few months, Long entered him into a tournament in the lightweight division. To everyone's surprise, he won. The competition wasn't topflight, and the title didn't lead to any future belts, but the experience stayed with Roosevelt and he boxed throughout his college career at Harvard. He was never a champion (even though he sparred with champions), but he was always game to fight. While Roosevelt's boxing career wasn't illustrious, it allowed for the rarest of opportunities: the chance for a normal guy to cold cock the leader of the free world without any repercussions.

One such incident involving a young artillery captain ultimately led to Roosevelt retiring from the sport for good. The event happened during a sparring session during his presidency. Once again, TR found himself in the ring with a man almost half his age. After holding his own for several rounds, the president missed landing a left hook on his opponent, and the young captain "cross countered [the president] on the eye, smashing the little blood vessels." Roosevelt's eye never healed properly, which meant the punch signaled the end of our most storied presidential pugilist's career.

Still, he lived for hand-to-hand combat and wrote this incredible letter to his sons about learning a new wrestling style:

> *I am very glad I have been doing this Japanese wrestling, but ... My right ankle and left wrist and one thumb and both great toes are swollen sufficiently to more or less impair their usefulness, and I am well mottled with bruises elsewhere. Still I have made good progress, and since you have left they have taught me three new throws that are perfect corkers.*

The "Tennis" Cabinet (a.k.a., the Iron Man Club)

Leave it to Teddy Roosevelt to take a simple tennis club and turn it into a precursor to the Ironman Triathlon. The "Tennis Cabinet" began early in Roosevelt's presidency as a group of men who, as the name would suggest, played tennis with the president in the afternoons. The crew started out innocently enough, but it wasn't long before TR decided that smacking a ball over a net with a racket for a few hours was tedious. Not only that, there was almost no risk for serious injury, which meant the thrill-seeking president wasn't getting his much-needed adrenaline rush to balance out the boring hours he had to log running the United States.

Pretty soon, the daily tennis sessions were replaced by what Roosevelt called "rough, cross-country walks," which would be like describing the Iditarod as a nice sleigh ride. In fact, these "walks" were nothing of the sort; they were obstacle courses in which the main goal was to push each man close to his physical limit. Some days the crew would hike down to the bottom of Rock Creek in Washington, D.C., and on others they'd trek across the Potomac River. The way they kept things interesting was to look at a map and randomly decide on a destination to hike to from the White House. They'd make a point of not researching whether there were any obstacles or bodies of water in the way, and they'd head out with the goal to not veer from the straight line to their destination for any reason.

This led to some hairy instances of scuffling down riverbeds, hikes over mountains, rock climbing, and perhaps most insanely of all, swimming across half-frozen rivers in the early spring and late fall. As if auditioning for a pre-Discovery Channel "President vs. Wild," our Bear Grylls-esque Commander-in-Chief often bragged that the routes he picked on these "rough cross-country walks" would force the men to swim through Rock Creek while "ice was floating thick upon it."

"Once I invited an entire class of officers who were attending lectures at the War College to come on one of these walks," Roosevelt says in his autobiography. "I chose a route which gave us the hardest climbing along the rocks and the deepest crossings of the creek; and my army friends enjoyed it hugely being the right sort, to a man."

WhAR (White House Athlete Ranking)

Executive Power

Looking at Roosevelt's rigorous physical activities, it was almost as if he was trying to prove on a daily basis that he was the strongest president. Boxing? Check. Wrestling? Check. Martial arts? Check. In fact, Roosevelt trained with world famous judo master Yoshiaki Yamashita, eventually rising to the level of brown belt. During his presidency, he was punched in the face, body slammed, submerged in a frozen river and shot — the first three voluntarily, the last one involuntarily. If surviving all four doesn't earn you a perfect 10 in the Executive Power rankings, nothing will.

SCORE: 10

Running Ability

Roosevelt was president about 80 years before the running and jogging craze of the 1980s, but he actively pursued his own version of both — only with obstacles in the way. TR scores well in this category, but a 10 is reserved for the absolute highest of fitness achievements. Only six presidents received a perfect score in this category, and while Roosevelt is at the top of the list, his sparring sessions fare slightly lower than running a marathon (George W. Bush), swimming 3 miles in the open ocean while dragging a wounded soldier (JFK), or being an All-American college football player (Gerald Ford). For once, TR will have to settle for being almost the best.

SCORE: 9.5

Fit for Office

No contest here. It would be hard to argue that a president sought out more physical activity while in office than TR. There's no need to go over his activities again, but it's safe to say that for modern presidents, Theodore Rex set the bar for exercise very, very high.

SCORE: 10

Executive Achievement

If a president got a trophy for activity level, Roosevelt would get a perfect score here again. Unfortunately, while he boxed in college, he never won a championship; and while he earned a brown belt in judo, he never competed for a title; and while he created torturous, triathlon-like obstacle courses, he never won any medals in a real competition. That's why he gets an 8 and not a 10. Only four presidents earned a 10 in this category. Ford earned his for being an NCAA All-American and football champion. George H.W. Bush earned his for playing in the college baseball World Series at Yale, twice. And Eisenhower got his 10 for earning a starting spot on the West Point football team as both a linebacker and a running back. Oh, and Hoover got a 10 for inventing his own sport — though it still wasn't enough to push him even near the top of this list.

SCORE: 8

Mettle of Honor

There's a fine line between toughness and strength. TR walked on both sides. His willingness to engage in hand-to-hand combat has already been established, but is there a greater measure of toughness than what he did after he was shot? Just before he was about to give a speech in Milwaukee, Roosevelt took a .32 caliber bullet to the chest at point blank range from a would-be assassin. Fortunately, he had some papers and a glasses case in his coat pocket that blunted the initial force of the impact. However, the bullet ended up lodged in the president's chest. After a short delay, TR went on to deliver his speech — with the bullet still in his body. After a few words, perhaps our manliest president pulled the bloodstained script of his speech from his chest pocket and said, "You see, it takes more than one bullet to kill a Bull Moose." He won over the crowd, and a solid 10 score for toughness in the process.

SCORE: 10

WhAR: 47.5

OVERALL RANKING: #2

Gerald Ford

HEIGHT: 6'
WEIGHT: 200
COLLEGE: Michigan
SPORTS: Football, Tennis, Golf

DESPITE CHEVY CHASE'S famous impression of Ford as a bumbling klutz on *Saturday Night Live*, the 38th president wins the award for the most athletically gifted of all our commanders-in-chief. Following an outstanding football career at Grand Rapids South High School in Michigan, where he was a captain and earned all-city honors, he earned a scholarship to the University of Michigan. As a Wolverine, he played center and linebacker for the team's back-to-back national championship teams in 1932 and '33, and then had his best individual season in 1934.

In 1932, the team went 8-0 and outscored its opponents 123-12 while completely shutting out six teams. The 1933 team also went undefeated, shut out five teams, and extended the team's unbeaten streak to 22 games (they did have one tie). Though the 1934 season saw the end of the winning streak after so many seniors had graduated, Ford had his best season and was named team MVP. He also made the 1935 Collegiate All-Star football team and played in an exhibition game against the Chicago Bears at Soldier Field. After graduation, Ford was good enough to be offered contracts by the Detroit Lions and the Green Bay Packers. Rather than play pro ball, however, Ford set his sights on attending Yale Law School, and he accepted positions as the Yale boxing coach and assistant varsity football coach.

When Ford entered the Navy during World War II, he worked briefly as a physical fitness instructor for pilots, thanks to his history of being an outstanding athlete.

After the war he took up tennis, golf and skiing. He was an excellent downhill skier and is affectionately known as the "First Citizen of Vail," as he started bringing his family there to ski in 1968, eventually building a house next to the Strawberry Lift at Beaver Creek. He even founded the Ford Cup, which eventually became the American Ski Classic.

As a lifelong golfer, Ford has a hole-in-one to his credit (on the fifth hole of the St. Jude Classic at Colonial Country Club in Memphis, Tennessee) — and unfortunately, several hit spectators. Though he could hit the ball a mile, he plunked enough fans off the tee box over the years to earn a reputation as a wild golfer. Even the legendary comedian and golfer Bob Hope got in on the action, once joking, "It's not hard to find Gerry Ford on the golf course... Just follow the wounded."

His No. 1 form of exercise in terms of volume while he was in office was swimming. He swam nearly every day in the White House and is the president responsible for putting in the outdoor pool that is still in use to this day. He was a decent freestyler, and the press occasionally were given access to the pool to grab a few photos of him doing laps.

WhAR (White House Athlete Ranking)

Executive Power

Gerald Ford was a big guy who excelled as an offensive lineman at the highest level of college football. While he doesn't have the feats of strength to match Washington, he likely had the same natural power, as he thrived in the trenches against other powerful young athletes.

SCORE: 10

Running Ability

Ford stayed in great shape throughout his life. He avoided running and a few other sports that would aggravate his knees, which were tender after his time in football. But between skiing, tennis, swimming and golf, he was easily one of our more active presidents throughout his life.

SCORE: 9

Fit for Office

While he was in office, he swam nearly every day, and he played a decent amount of golf and some tennis. It wasn't quite the same regimen as our exercise over-achievers like Teddy Roosevelt, Bush and Obama, but it's still more than almost every other POTUS.

SCORE: 9.5

Executive Achievement

Like Bush 41, we're giving a 10 here for winning back-to-back national championships in Division-I college football and for getting offers to play in the pros.

SCORE: 10

Mettle of Honor

When measuring the toughest positions to play in football, center will likely be at the top of the list, and Gerald Ford was a team MVP. He also served with distinction in World War II onboard the light aircraft carrier Monterey in the Pacific Theater.

SCORE: 10

WhAR: 48.5

OVERALL RANKING: #1

Acknowledgements

This truly is the first book in the history of history writing that exclusively covers the athletic talents of every single United States president. That being the case, for about one-third to one-half of our presidents, there was no previous research or basis for gauging how athletic or fit a commander-in-chief was. In many instances, information that was pertinent to a president's sports skill was out there, but it was buried in a biography that was long out-of-print or in personal papers revealed on a president's official website or even, in one case, discovered in a photo tour of the president's once-lived-in house.

Whenever I encountered a dead end or got frustrated with not finding any athletic, fitness or exercise information about an Oval Office occupant, I thought of my favorite history writers and how they spent years of their lives focusing on one president or one period of a presidency at a time.

I'd like to acknowledge some of my favorite history authors here: Candice Millard, David McCullough, Joseph J. Ellis, Ron Chernow, Richard Brookhiser, Stephen E. Ambrose, Doris Kearns Goodwin and Robert Kurson

I'm sure I'm leaving people out but those are the excellent writers who come to mind.

I also have to thank the University of Virginia's Miller Center, which is an invaluable resource when it comes to researching a president's life and time in office. WhiteHouse.gov, History.com and Biography.com are all close seconds, and of course, Wikipedia is phenomenal for not only basic presidential info, but also the sources cited on each president's page provided new avenues for research.

Magazines like *Sports Illustrated, Time, Parade* and several other larger national publications wrote a smattering of stories over the years on some of the modern presidents' physical pursuits and they were valuable resources. Since so many modern presidents took up golf (willingly and unwillingly), *Golf Week* and *Golf Digest* were also very helpful. It seems silly to thank Google, but realistically, writing this book twenty-five years ago would have required an absurd number of hours traveling and lots of time on the phone with historians and in libraries poring over micro-film and digging through encyclopedias. Because of Google, I was able to knock out a vast majority of the research on our more obscure presidents from my own couch.

That is not something I take for granted, so thanks, Google!

I really want to thank Jeanine Henning for her amazing illustrations of the presidents and for the cover design. We have worked together on several books and she always seems to "get" the images I have in my mind and draw the perfectly. Thank you!

And thanks also to Jared Evans, who has been editing my word salad since we first met at *Muscle & Fitness* well over a decade ago.

And thank you, the reader. This topic has fascinated me for a long time and if you've gotten this far, it fascinates you, too. I hope you learned as much reading this book as I did writing it.

Jon

References (Listed in Alphabetical Order by President)

John Adams

BusinessInsider.com: https://www.businessinsider.com/john-adams-daily-routine-2017-7

John Adams, McCullough, David G. Published: New York : Simon & Schuster, 2002. Edition: 1st Touchstone ed.

John Quincy Adams

BusinessInsider.com: https://www.businessinsider.com/john-quincy-adams-skinny-dipping-routine-2017-2

New England Historical Society: http://www.newenglandhistoricalsociety.com/7-fun-facts-john-quincy-adams/

ShannonSelin.com: https://shannonselin.com/2017/07/john-quincy-adams-swimming/

Chester A. Arthur

MentalFloss.com: http://mentalfloss.com/article/68824/8-things-you-might-not-know-about-chester-arthur

MillerCenter.org: https://millercenter.org/president/arthur/life-before-the-presidency

Time Magazine: http://content.time.com/time/specials/packages/article/0,28804,1879648_1879646_1879694,00.html

James Buchanan

LancasterHistory.org: https://www.lancasterhistory.org/president-buchanans-drinking-habits/

WhiteHouse.gov: https://www.whitehouse.gov/about-the-white-house/presidents/james-buchanan/

George H. W. Bush

Forbes: https://www.forbes.com/sites/monteburke/2018/12/01/george-h-w-bush-was-the-most-sporting-president-in-u-s-history/#121b7b2f220f

SABR.org: https://sabr.org/research/complete-collegiate-baseball-record-george-hw-bush

Soccer America: https://www.socceramerica.com/publications/article/80613/george-bush-presidential-center-forward-and-scori.html

Sports Illustrated: https://www.si.com/more-sports/2018/12/04/george-hw-bush-41st-president-sports-obituary-yale-baseball-sportsmanship

USA Today: https://www.usatoday.com/story/sports/2018/12/01/george-hw-bush-love-baseball-dating-back-days-yale/2171698002/

Washington Post: https://www.washingtonpost.com/sports/george-hw-bush-had-a-love-of-sports-and-an-affinity-for-at-least-one-sportswriter/2018/12/01/328a2e66-f5b0-11e8-80d0-f7e1948d55f4_story.html

George W. Bush

Fox Sports: https://www.foxsports.com/buzzer/gallery/the-10-most-athletic-presidents-ranked-110816

History.com: https://www.history.com/news/us-presidents-athletes

Men's Health: https://www.menshealth.com/fitness/a19537999/fittest-american-presidents/

Runners World: https://www.runnersworld.com/runners-stories/a20820870/report-likely-overstates-george-w-bushs-running-prowess/

Sports Illustrated: https://www.si.com/edge/2016/07/08/weekender-george-w-bush-70th-birthday-mountain-biking

The Guardian: https://www.theguardian.com/world/2008/novd/07/us-elections-2008-barack-obama

Jimmy Carter

Runners World: https://www.runnersworld.com/advanced/a20836257/jimmy-carters-first-road-race/

SportsIllustrated.com (this really is the shortest link, sorry):

https://www.si.com/vault/1979/09/24/823995/jimmy-carter-runs-into-the-wall-it-happens--sudden-utter-exhaustion--to-a-lot-of-inexperienced-road-runners-who-try-too-hard-too-soon-but-when-the-tottering-competitor-happens-to-be-the-president-of-the-united-states-it-can-be-a

WashingtonPost.com: https://www.washingtonpost.com/
national/health-science/jimmy-carter-now-88-on-aging-
and-health/2013/05/03/84f67db8-9ae8-11e2-9bda-ed-
d1a7fb557d_story.html

Grover Cleveland

ConstitutionCenter.org: https://constitutioncenter.org/
blog/10-fascinating-facts-about-grover-cleveland-the-on-
ly-double-president

Fitness Magazine: https://www.fitnessmagazine.com/health/
americas-10-unhealthiest-presidents/

MillerCenter.org: https://millercenter.org/president/cleveland/
life-before-the-presidency

Bill Clinton

CNN.com: https://www.cnn.com/2015/01/22/politics/bill-clin-
ton-sports-glory-days/index.html

Saturday Night Live, Phil Hartman, Bill Clinton to McDonald's
skit: https://www.youtube.com/watch?v=eYt0khR_ej0

USNews.com: https://www.usnews.com/news/blogs/washing-
ton-whispers/2012/02/29/bill-clintons-running-habit-a-se-
cret-service-nightmare

Calvin Coolidge

Baseball-Almanac.com: https://www.baseball-almanac.com/
prz_ccc.shtml

CoolidgeFoundation.org: https://www.coolidgefoundation.org/

Ducksters.com: https://www.ducksters.com/biography/uspresidents/calvincoolidge.php

Washington Post: https://www.washingtonpost.com/news/animalia/wp/2018/04/03/the-brief-history-of-a-widely-mocked-electric-horse-in-the-white-house/

Washington Post: http://www.washingtonpost.com/wpsrv/style/guideposts/fitness/post/presidents.htm?noredirect=on

Dwight Eisenhower

DwightEisenhower.com: https://www.dwightdeisenhower.com/194/Sports

GolfWeek.com: https://golfweek.com/2009/11/02/dwight-d-eisenhower-golf-white-house/

SportofHistory.com: http://www.sportofhistory.com/which-us-presidents-football-career-was-ended-by-jim-thorpe/

MLB.com: https://www.mlb.com/cut4/presidents-day-dwight-eisenhowers-baseball-career/c-215884914

MillerCenter.org: https://millercenter.org/president/eisenhower/life-in-brief

Millard Fillmore

WhiteHouse.gov: https://www.whitehouse.gov/about-the-white-house/presidents/millard-fillmore/

MillerCenter.org: https://millercenter.org/president/fillmore

Gerald Ford

Bleacher Report: https://bleacherreport.com/articles/1218861-michigan-football-gerald-fords-legendary-number-48-getting-un-retired

SkiingHistory.org: https://www.skiinghistory.org/lives/jerry-ford

Swimming World: https://www.swimmingworldmagazine.com/news/the-presidential-history-of-swimming/

Vanity Fair: https://www.vanityfair.com/news/2012/09/most-athletic-presidents-of-all-time

James Garfield

Biography.com: https://www.biography.com/us-president/james-garfield

Destiny of the Republic, Candice Millard, Anchor Books, 2012

Ulysses S. Grant

Grant Home Page: https://www.granthomepage.com/grantequestrian.htm

Miller Center: https://millercenter.org/president/grant/life-before-the-presidency

WestPointCivilWar.com: https://westpointcivilwar.wordpress.

com/2011/03/26/did-you-know-ulysses-s-grant-was-a-horse-whisperer/

Warren G. Harding

Time Magazine: http://content.time.com/time/specials/packages/article/0,28804,1879648_1879646_1879696,00.html

Wikipedia.org: https://en.wikipedia.org/wiki/Warren_G._Harding_High_School

WhiteHouse.Gov: https://www.whitehouse.gov/about-the-white-house/presidents/warren-g-harding/

Benjamin Harrison

Benjamin Harrison Home website: https://bhpsite.org/

MillerCenter.org: https://millercenter.org/president/bharrison

NPS.org: https://www.nps.gov/nr/travel/presidents/benjamin_harrison_home.html

William Henry Harrison

Biography.com: https://www.biography.com/us-president/william-henry-harrison

MillerCenter.org: https://millercenter.org/president/harrison

WhiteHouse.gov: https://www.whitehouse.gov/about-the-white-house/presidents/william-henry-harrison/

Rutherford B. Hayes

RBHayes.org: https://www.rbhayes.org/main/ruther-ford-b.-hayes/

HarvardLaw.edu: https://today.law.harvard.edu/hlss-first-alum-nus-elected-as-president-rutherford-b-hayes/

Herbert Hoover

HooverArchives.gov: https://hoover.archives.gov/hoovers/history-hoover-ball

Wbur.org: https://www.wbur.org/onlyagame/2016/03/05/hoover-ball-crossfit-president-politics

WhiteHouseHistory.gov: https://www.whitehousehistory.org/president-herbert-hoover-and-baseball

Andrew Jackson

MillerCenter.org: https://millercenter.org/president/jackson

TheHermitage.com: https://thehermitage.com/learn/andrew-jackson/president/

Thomas Jefferson

American Sphinx, Ellis, Joseph J, Published: New York: Random House 1998

Monticello.org: https://www.monticello.org/site/research-and-collections/exercise

Andrew Johnson

Baseball-Almanac.com: https://www.baseball-almanac.com/
prz_qaj.shtml

History.com: https://www.history.com/topics/us-presidents/
andrew-johnson

MillerCenter.org: https://millercenter.org/president/johnson

Lyndon B. Johnson

Baseball-Reference.com: https://www.baseballreference.com/
bullpen/Lyndon_B._Johnson

HHS.gov: https://www.hhs.gov/fitness/about-pcsfn/our-his-
tory/index.html

LBJLibrary.org: http://www.lbjlibrary.org/lyndon-baines-john-
son/lbj-biography

MillerCenter.org: https://millercenter.org/president/lbjohnson

John F. Kennedy

Pro Football Hall of Fame: https://www.profootballhof.com/
presidents-who-played-football/

Sports Illustrated: https://www.si.com/more-sports/pho-
tos/2013/11/22/john-f-kennedy-and-sports

TheCrimson.com: https://www.thecrimson.com/arti-
cle/1970/10/21/harvard-coaches-recall-kennedy-as-frail/

WhiteHouseHistory.org: https://www.whitehousehistory.org/
presidents-and-college-football

Abraham Lincoln

AbrahamLincolnsClassroom.org: http://www.abrahamlincoln-
sclassroom.org/abraham-lincoln-in-depth/abraham-lin-
coln-the-athlete/

Fightland.Vice.com: http://fightland.vice.com/blog/the-street-
fighting-life-of-abraham-lincoln

History.com: https://www.history.com/news/10-things-you-
may-not-know-about-abraham-lincoln

Sports Illustrated (SI.com): https://www.si.com/extra-mus-
tard/2013/02/12/abraham-lincoln-was-a-skilled-wrestler-
and-world-class-trash-talker

Weekly View: http://weeklyview.net/2018/09/20/the-abra-
ham-lincoln-handball/

James Madison

Britannica.org: https://www.britannica.com/biography/
James-Madison

BusinessInsider.com: https://www.businessinsider.com/
james-madison-daily-routine-2017-7

Montpelier.org: https://www.montpelier.org/learn/the-life-of-
james-madison

William McKinley

CantonRep.com: https://www.cantonrep.com/article/20120924/
NEWS/309249857

Physical Culture, Vol. 12, Physical Culture Publishing Company,
Bernarr MacFadden Editor-In-Chief, Page 312

VisitCanton.com https://www.visitcanton.com/blog/stark11-11-
facts-about-president-mckinley-you-may-not-know/

James Monroe

MillerCenter.org: https://millercenter.org/president/monroe/
domestic-affairs

PloddingThroughPresidents.com: https://www.plod-
dingthroughthepresidents.com/2016/10/10-things-james-
monroe-loved.html

Richard Nixon

Baseball-Almanac.com: https://www.baseball-almanac.com/
prz_qrn.shtml

MillerCenter.org: https://millercenter.org/president/nixon

NixonFoundation.org: https://www.nixonfoundation.
org/2014/04/love-game-rn-baseball/

Barack Obama

Golf Digest: https://www.golfdigest.com/story/

weve-crunched-the-numbers-and-its-official-president-
obama-played-a-lot-of-golf-while-in-office

For The Win – *USA Today*: https://ftw.usatoday.
com/2017/01/
president-barack-obama-basketball-how-good-arne-dun-
can-photos-videos

Los Angeles Times: https://www.latimes.com/archives/la-xpm-
2008-nov-10-sp-crowe10-story.html

Franklin Pierce

MillerCenter.org: https://millercenter.org/president/pierce

WhiteHouse.gov: https://www.whitehouse.gov/about-the-
white-house/presidents/franklin-pierce/

James K. Polk

JamesKPolk.com: http://www.jameskpolk.com/james-polk-bi-
ography.php

WhiteHouse.gov: https://www.whitehouse.gov/about-the-
white-house/presidents/james-k-polk/

Ronald Reagan

Chicago Tribune: https://www.chicagotribune.com/news/ct-ron-
ald-reagan-lifeguard-statue-met-20170104-story.html

Parade.com: https://parade.com/116185/ronaldreagan/16-rea-
gan-fitness/

ReaganLibrary.gov: https://www.reaganlibrary.gov/sreference/
military-service-of-ronald-reagan

International Swimming Hall of Fame Site: https://ishof.org/
ronald-reagan.html

Franklin Delano Roosevelt

FDRLibrary.org: https://www.fdrlibrary.org/fdr-facts

FDRFoundation.org: https://fdrfoundation.org/the-fdr-suite/
franklin-roosevelt-at-harvard/

WhiteHouseHistory.org: https://www.whitehousehistory.org/
questions/does-the-white-house-have-a-pool

Theodore Roosevelt

Brazilian Jiu-Jitsu World: https://bjj-world.com/theodore-roos-
evelts-training-wrestling-vs-jiu-jitsu/

Bleacher Report: https://bleacherreport.com/arti-
cles/2559772-theodore-roosevelt-the-rough-and-tum-
ble-wrestling-grappling-president

Fightland.Vice.Com: http://fightland.vice.com/blog/the-strenu-
ous-life-theodore-roosevelts-mixed-martial-arts

Men's Health: https://www.menshealth.com/fitness/a19532389/
presidential-fitness-secrets/

Theodore Roosevelt Center: https://www.theodorerooseveltcen-
ter.org/Blog/Item/Theodore-san

US Sports History: https://ussporthistory.com/2016/11/21/
    sparring-in-the-white-house-theodore-roosevelt-race-and-
    boxing/

William Howard Taft

Bivins, Roberta; Marland, Hilary (2016). "Weighting for Health:
    Management, Measurement and Self-surveillance in the
    Modern Household". Social History of Medicine. 29 (4):
    757–780.

ConstitutionCenter.org: https://constitutioncenter.org/
    blog/10-fascinating-facts-about-president-and-chief-jus-
    tice-william-howard-taft-

History.com: https://www.history.com/news/did-william-how-
    ard-taft-really-get-stuck-in-a-bathtub

Plarr, Victor, ed. (1899)."Yorke-Davies, Nathaniel Edwards".
    Men and Women of the Time: A Dictionary of Contempo-
    raries (15th ed.). London: George Routledge & Sons. p.
    1203.

Sotos, John G. (September 2003). "Taft and Pickwick". Chest.
    124(3): 1133–1142 Pringle vol. 2, pp. 963–964, 1072.

Zachary Taylor

Biography.com: https://www.biography.com/us-president/zach-
    ary-taylor

MillerCenter.org: https://millercenter.org/president/taylor/
    death-of-the-president

Harry Truman

TrumanLittleWhiteHouse.com: https://www.trumanlittlewhite-house.com/guide/the-daily-schedule

TrumanLibrary.com: https://www.trumanlibrary.gov/library/truman-papers

WhiteHouse.gov: https://www.whitehouse.gov/about-the-white-house/presidents/harry-s-truman/

Donald Trump

Business Insider.com: https://www.businessinsider.com/donald-trump-high-school-classmates-what-he-was-like-2015-10

Pro Football Hall of Fame: https://www.profootballhof.com/presidents-who-played-football/

President Golf Tracker: https://presidentialgolftracker.com/trump-vs-obama-golf-games/

12up.com: https://www.12up.com/posts/4108954-6-things-you-didn-t-know-about-donald-trump-s-baseball-career

John Tyler

MillerCenter.org: https://millercenter.org/president/tyler

WhiteHouse.gov: https://www.whitehouse.gov/about-the-white-house/presidents/john-tyler/

Martin Van Buren

Britannica.com: https://www.britannica.com/biography/Martin-Van-Buren

Josh Gulch.com: http://www.joshgulch.com/gopher/themes/mvb.html

Senate.gov: https://www.senate.gov/artandhistory/history/common/generic/VP_Martin_VanBuren.htm

George Washington

Health, Fitness Revolution: https://www.healthfitnessrevolution.com/top-10-health-fitness-tips-george-washington/

His Excellency, Ellis, Joseph J., Vintage, Reprint Edition, 2005

MountVernon.org: https://www.mountvernon.org/george-washington/facts/washington-stories/remarkably-robust-and-athletic-george-washington-the-sportsman/

National Wrestling Hall of Fame: https://nwhof.org/stillwater/resources-library/history/wrestling-in-the-usa/

NPCCoin.com: https://www.ngccoin.com/boards/topic/123308-did-george-washington-really-throw-a-silver-dollar-across-the-potomac-river/

Woodrow Wilson

Adventure Cycling: https://www.adventurecycling.org/blog/woodrow-wilson-cyclist/

Sports Illustrated: https://www.si.com/vault/1962/07/16/600615/
    the-scholarly-sportsman

WilsonCenter.org: https://www.wilsoncenter.org/about-wood-
    row-wilson

General References on the Athletic Ability of Presidents

BusinessInsider.com: https://www.businessinsider.
    com/trump-exercise-president-workout-rou-
    tines-obama-bush-clinton-2018-2

Mashable.com: https://mashable.com/2017/02/18/cabinet-exer-
    cises/

Men's Health.com: https://www.menshealth.com/fitness/
    a19537999/fittest-american-presidents/

Mental Floss: https://mentalfloss.com/article/73533/healthy-
    habits-15-us-presidents

RealClearSports.com: http://www.realclearsports.com/lists/
    top_10_least_athletic_presidents/calvin_coolidge.html

Self Magazine: https://www.self.com/gallery/former-us-presi-
    dents-exercise-habits

Our White House: http://ourwhitehouse.org/stress-relief-exer-
    cise-and-relaxation-at-the-white-house/

The Official Ranking of the Most Athletic Presidents

	Executive Power	Running Ability	Fit for Office	Executive Experience	Mettle of Honor	WH.A.R. TOTAL	RANKS
1 - Gerald Ford	10	9	9.5	10	10	48.5	1
2 - Theodore Roosevelt	10	9.5	10	8	10	47.5	2
3 - George Washington	10	8	6	10	10	44	3
4 - George Bush	7	10	7.5	10	10	43.5	4
5 - Abraham Lincoln	10	8	6	9	10	43	5
6 - George W. Bush	8	10	10	9	5	42	6
7 - John F. Kennedy	8	7	6	10	10	41	7
8 - Dwight Eisenhower	7.5	7	7	9	10	40.5	8
9 - Ronald Reagan	7	10	9	7	7	40	9
10 - Barack Obama	7	9	10	8	5	39	10
11 - James A. Garfield	10	6	2	7	10	35	11
12 - Jimmy Carter	4	8	7	10	5	34	12
13 - Herbert Hoover	6	6	10	9	2.5	33.5	13
14 - James Monroe	7	5	3	3	10	28	14
15 - Ulysses S. Grant	5	3	3	5	10	26	15
16 - Rutherford Hayes	6	5	3	5	6	25	16
17 - Franklin Roosevelt	5	5	5	3.5	6	24.5	17
18 - Zachary Taylor	6	6	2	5.5	7	24	18
19 - John Q. Adams	4	5	7.5	3	4	23.5	19
20 - Andrew Jackson	5	5	3	3	7	23	20
21 - William McKinley	5	4	3	4.5	6	22.5	21

	Executive Power	Running Ability	Fit for Office	Executive Experience	Mettle of Honor	WH.A.R. TOTAL	RANKS
22 - Woodrow Wilson	2	6	5	5	4	22	22
23 - William H. Harrison	6	6	0	3.5	7	21.5	23
24 - Donald Trump	5	3	3	5	3	19	24
25 - William H. Taft	5	3	4	3	3	18	25
26 - Harry S. Truman	3	2	5	2.5	5	17.5	26
27 - Richard Nixon	3	3	3	5	3	17	27
28 - Lyndon Johnson	6	2	2	2.5	4	16.5	28
29 - Thomas Jefferson	3	4	3.5	2.5	3	16	29
30 - Bill Clinton	5	2	5.5	2	1	15.5	30
31 - Millard Fillmore	2	2	2	2.5	6	14.5	31
32 - Chester Arthur	5	3	1	2	3	14	32
33 - Calvin Coolidge	2	3	5	2.5	1	13.5	33
34 - Benjamin Harrison	2	1	1.5	2.5	6	13	34
35 - John Adams	2	2.5	1	1	3	9.5	35
36 - Franklin Pierce	3	1	1	1	3	9	36
37 - James Buchanan	2.5	1	1	1	3	8.5	37
38 - Grover Cleveland	5	1	1	1	0	8	38
39 - Warren G. Harding	3.5	1	1	1	1	7.5	39
40 - James Madison	1	1	1	1	3	7	40
41 - John Tyler	1	1	1.5	2	1	6.5	41
42 - Andrew Johnson	1	1	1	2	1	6	42
43 - Martin Van Buren	1	1	1	1	1.5	5.5	43
44 - James K. Polk	1	1	1	1	1	5	44

Did You Like This Book?

Please let everyone know by posting a review on Amazon. Just type the below link into your browser and it will take you directly to the reviews page: http://amzn.to/1SWEhWA

Please visit www.jonfinkel.com to send me any questions or for information on my other books or media appearances.

Sign up for my newsletter here: http://www.jonfinkel.com/newsletter/

Thank you for reading!

About the Author

Jon Finkel's books have been endorsed by everyone from Tony Dungy and Spike Lee to Chef Robert Irvine and Mark Cuban. He is the author of *The Life of Dad: Reflections on Fatherhood from Today's Leaders, Icons and Legendary Dads* and *The Athlete: Greatness, Grace and the Unprecedented Life of Charlie Ward* on Heisman Trophy winner, National Champion and New York Knicks star, Charlie Ward.

He also wrote *"Mean" Joe Greene: Built By Football* with 4x Super Bowl Champion Joe Greene, *Heart Over Height* with 3x NBA Dunk Champion Nate Robinson and *Forces of Character* with 3x Super Bowl Champion and Fighter Pilot Chad Hennings. In addition, he authored the Mario Lopez-endorsed fatherhood fitness book, *The Dadvantage.*

As a feature writer, he has written for *Men's Health*, Men's Fitness, *The New York Times, GQ, Details, Yahoo! Sports* and many more. His NBA book series, *Greatest Stars of the NBA* won several American Library Association awards and the twelve books were a part of the NBA's famous "Read to Achieve" program. His feature writing also received a notable mention in the 2015 Best American Sports Writing Anthology.

Jon has been a live TV guest on *CBS: This Morning* and *Good Morning Texas* and has appeared on hundreds of radio stations, podcasts and live-streams promoting his work.

He is also the co-host of the *Life of Dad Show* podcast (600k downloads) and the *Lunch Break Facebook Live Show* (1M viewers).

Made in the USA
Middletown, DE
23 December 2023

46717883R00128